AS/A-Level Student Text Guide

Anne Crow

Series Editor: Marian Cox

Doctor Faustus

Christopher Marlowe

Philip Allan Updates, an imprint of Hodder Education, an Hachette UK company, Market Place, Deddington, Oxfordshire OX15 0SE

Orders

Bookpoint Ltd, 130 Milton Park, Abingdon, Oxfordshire OX14 4SB
tel: 01235 827827
fax: 01235 400401
e-mail: education@bookpoint.co.uk
Lines are open 9.00 a.m.–5.00 p.m., Monday to Saturday, with a 24-hour message answering service. You can also order through the Philip Allan Updates website: www.philipallan.co.uk

© Philip Allan Updates 2010

ISBN 978-0-340-98784-1

First printed 2010
Impression number 5 4 3
Year 2014 2013 2012 2011

Printed by MPG Books, Bodmin

Hachette UK's policy is to use papers that are natural, renewable and recyclable products and made from wood grown in sustainable forests. The logging and manufacturing processes are expected to conform to the environmental regulations of the country of origin.

P01780

Contents

Introduction

Aims of the guide

The purpose of this guide is to enable you to organise your thoughts and responses to the play, to deepen your understanding of key features and aspects, and finally to help you to address the particular requirements of examination questions and coursework assignments. It is assumed that you have read and studied the play already under the guidance of a teacher or lecturer. This Student Text Guide is a revision guide, not an introduction, although some of its content serves the purpose of providing initial background.

The *Text Guidance* consists of a series of chapters that examine key aspects of the text including contexts, interpretations and controversies. Terms defined in 'Literary terms and concepts' are highlighted the first time they appear in this section. *Questions and Answers* gives examples of essay questions of different types and includes exemplar essay plans and sample essays. Note that the examiners are seeking above all else evidence of an *informed personal response* to the text. A revision guide such as this can help you to understand the text and to form your own opinions, and it can suggest areas to think about, but it cannot replace your own ideas and responses as an individual reader.

This guide is based on the A-text, as that is the one used in most modern editions. Line references to the text are to the 2009 Oxford University Press edition.

Assessment Objectives

The revised Assessment Objectives for A-level English Literature from 2008 are common to all boards:

AO1	Articulate creative, informed and relevant responses to literary texts, using appropriate terminology and concepts, and coherent, accurate written expression.
AO2	Demonstrate detailed critical understanding in analysing the ways in which structure, form and language shape meaning in literary texts.
AO3	Explore connections and comparisons between different literary texts, informed by the interpretation of other readers.
AO4	Demonstrate understanding of the significance and influence of the contexts in which literary texts are written and received.

Text Guidance

Contexts

Marlowe's birthplace: Canterbury

Unlike William Shakespeare, who grew up in the provincial market town of Stratford-upon-Avon, Marlowe was born in Canterbury, a bustling, cosmopolitan city with a turbulent history. Ever since Augustine settled there to convert the pagan English to Christianity, Canterbury has been the religious capital of England. In AD 1170, Thomas Becket, Archbishop of Canterbury, was brutally murdered in the cathedral. He was declared a traitor, and royal troops occupied the city. His bloodstained clothes were distributed to the poor; six days after he died a woman named Britheva claimed to have miraculously recovered her sight after touching one of these items.

Becket was soon venerated as a martyr, and, barely three years after his death, he was canonised by Pope Alexander III. Canterbury became a centre of pilgrimage throughout Europe as more and more miracles were recorded, and the city prospered. The Church in Kent grew wealthy and came to own nearly half of Kentish land. Tension grew between Church and state as Canterbury's burgesses challenged monks over the rights of pasture, rights of sanctuary, taxes and boundary walls. Then Henry VIII decided to erase all evidence of the Papacy, declared St Thomas a rebel and a traitor, and had his shrine removed. In March 1539, 26 wagon-loads of gold and jewels were carried away from the cathedral by Henry's men. Less than 20 years later, his Catholic daughter, Mary, took measures to restore Roman Catholicism and had 41 Protestants burned for heresy just outside Canterbury's walls.

When Christopher Marlowe was born on 26 February 1564, just two months before the birth of William Shakespeare, Elizabeth was on the throne, and England was once again Protestant. His father, John, was a poor but hard-working and ambitious apprentice cobbler from a coastal village. Two months after Christopher's birth, John was made 'free' of the city and thus able to set up his own establishment and join the local shoemakers' guild. Young Christopher would have watched the gentlemen in their elaborate dress, swords by their sides, as they came to buy the latest fashions in footwear. The city was very busy, packed with people from all walks of life, many of whom came from outside the city, like Chaucer's fictional pilgrims, or even from abroad, to venerate St Thomas à Becket. Mingling among the large crowds would have been pedlars, minstrels, jugglers and other street performers.

A bustling, noisy city

As well as street entertainment, Canterbury has a long theatrical tradition. Before the dissolution of the monasteries, it was an offence for a craftsman not to act in

one of the Corpus Christi mystery plays. In Marlowe's day there were plenty of itinerant acting troupes to be watched in the inns and the churches, and mayoral elections were accompanied by satires, slogans and brief, irreverent plays. He would undoubtedly have watched the anti-Catholic skits that were often acted in the city's churches.

The cathedral with its elaborate carvings and gargoyles dominated the walled city. Even the ordinary buildings would have fascinated an imaginative child with their wooden carvings of grotesque devils, angels, and dragons, some of which survive to this day. It was a violent age; even a game of football was likely to prove fatal, as Philip Stubbs declared in *The Anatomy of Abuses* (1583): 'I protest unto you that it may rather be called a friendly kind of fight than a play or recreation — a bloody and murdering practice than a fellowly sport or pastime.' The city's council, or Burghmote, had decreed that beef could not be sold unless the animals were subjected to a public baiting, so Marlowe could have frequently watched scenes of bull-baiting, as well as public hangings. A public execution was an event not to be missed and people would queue through the night to get the best places; there was always a carnival atmosphere, and pie sellers, ale merchants and souvenir sellers did excellent business.

School

Both of Marlowe's parents could read and write, and they were ambitious for their son to receive the best education Canterbury had to offer. Four of the Marlowes' nine children were male, but two died early, so Christopher was the only son until he was 12. He received a basic education at a 'petty' school (from the French *petit*), where he would have learned arithmetic, and reading and writing would have been taught through the Lord's Prayer and the catechism. He would have been subjected to lectures such as *A Homily against Disobedience and Wilful Rebellion*, published in 1570, which stated that all protest was wicked; disobedience is 'the worst of all vices', 'the greatest of all mischiefs'. From an early age he would have been indoctrinated with the teaching that he was later to question through his anti-hero, Doctor Faustus. After petty school, like Shakespeare, he was probably sent to grammar school, at which he would have been introduced to the classics. He was evidently very able and hard-working at school because he was awarded a scholarship to the King's School in January 1579.

The King's School claims to be the world's oldest extant school, founded in AD 597 by St Augustine as a cathedral school. Here Marlowe would have been allowed to speak no language other than Latin or Greek. Poetry and original composition were on the curriculum. Pupils had to memorise rules for writing poetry and be skilled at translating Latin poetry as well as writing their own verse in Latin. They learned to compose speeches and to 'make varyings of speech in every mood'. They had to write *controversiae*, arguing for both sides of a debate, and *imitatio*,

borrowing phrases from various sources to create a powerful new speech. The headmaster, John Gresshop, was an erudite and well-read man with very broad tastes. He clearly loved books because when he died, in Marlowe's fifth term, he left more than 350 volumes, which would have been a huge library at that time. Gresshop having no living relative, the books were catalogued and probably made available for the students to read outside class.

Gresshop's books were not all concerned with religion; he also owned copies of Latin comedies by Terence and Plautus, a copy of erotic poems by Théodore de Bèze, and some lurid prints. Marlowe was doubtless introduced to the sexually explicit Roman poet Ovid, whose *Amores* he translated early in his writing career. He would also have met Lucan's *Pharsalia*, which contained dramatic dialogues such as that between Menippus and Hermes in the underworld. When Hermes points out the skull of Helen of Troy, Menippus asks with cool **irony**, 'Was it then for this that the thousand ships were manned from all Greece, for this so many Greeks and barbarians fell, and so many cities were devastated?' Marlowe echoes this speech with Faustus's reaction to Helen of Troy: 'Was this the face that launched a thousand ships?'

This education was invaluable training for a playwright, and drama did have a lively history at the school. The boys only needed the approval of a master and they were free from the attentions of the official censor. Some people attribute to Marlowe a play called *Timon*, written by one or more of the pupils, which mocked Drake's great world voyage from which he returned in 1580. In that year, Marlowe left the city to go to Cambridge University.

Life and works of Christopher Marlowe

Watching or reading *Doctor Faustus*, we come to the inescapable conclusion that Christopher Marlowe had a lively, enquiring mind, a restless adventurous spirit, and was well versed in theological debates. Marlowe was from the same social class as Shakespeare, but Marlowe had the benefit of a university education. He was awarded one of only three Archbishop Parker scholarships to Corpus Christi College, Cambridge. Recipients of this honour had to be 'forward in learning, and also well-minded in the service of God', but did not at first have to prepare for the Church. Marlowe had won his award partly for his musical ability and skill in making verses. At university there were strict rules about dress; students had to wear a long drab gown and a skullcap. We can guess that Marlowe resented this because one of Faustus's ambitions is to 'fill the public schools with silk,/ Wherewith the students shall be bravely clad' (1.1.92–93).

Marlowe was formally admitted in 1581, at the age of 17, so he would have been older than many of the other students as the university statutes stipulated 14 as the minimum age for a scholar. His scholarship was initially to allow him to prepare for a Bachelor of Arts degree, with the possibility of an extension to enable him to proceed to become a Master of Arts. The curriculum was largely based around the study of grammar, **rhetoric** and dialectic, together known as the 'trivium'. Examinations were oral rather than written, so Marlowe would have had plenty of practice at both defending and attacking a particular propo-sition in a dialectic in front of an audience. Credit was given for facility and fluency, as well as for the selection and arrangement of material, so this was excellent training for a playwright whose characters were to suggest and support unorthodox opinions.

It was customary for students to have their portrait painted when they achieved their degree, and a portrait that is presumed to be of Marlowe was painted in 1585, when he was 21. When we study this portrait, we can gain a feel of the man behind the plays. He is dressed in the height of fashion in a padded black velvet doublet, slashed to reveal flame-coloured silk underneath. The simple collar is of 'cobweb lawn', and bossed gold buttons run down its front and along the sleeves. One arm is folded confidently over the other, and the brown eyes seem to challenge the observer. The motto in the top left-hand corner could be Faustus's own: *quod me nutrit me destruit* ('that which nourishes me, destroys me'). Just as Marlowe was destroyed by his unguarded tongue and his reckless craving for excitement and adventure, so Faustus was destroyed by his reckless craving for knowledge and power.

Espionage

The portrait and the flamboyant doublet would have been too expensive for a poor student on a scholarship, but we can tell from the records of the Corpus Christi College buttery that, once Marlowe had been awarded his BA degree and was studying for his MA, he had more money to spend. It is most probable that the extra funds he was flaunting with the portrait and in the buttery came from working as a spy for Sir Francis Walsingham, head of Queen Elizabeth's secret service. Students at Cambridge were often recruited by one of Walsingham's agents, and the young scholar and playwright with an enquiring mind would have been a useful asset.

His frequent absences from the university, which are generally assumed to be because of his work as a spy, led the university authorities to refuse to award him the degree of Master of Arts, even though he had fulfilled the requirements. Most students at Cambridge at this time went into the priesthood. Those who intended to become Catholic priests would leave shortly before they took their MA and defect to the English college at Rheims. Here they would be trained for their secret ministry before returning to England to risk a traitor's death. It is conjectured that Marlowe was probably set to spy on these traitors from the inside, because a letter from the Queen's Privy Council overturned the decision of the university authorities.

Under the terms of his scholarship, Marlowe would have had to give assurance to the college that he intended to enter the Church. However, the MA programme was not concerned with divinity; the emphasis was on classical philosophy, which included related subjects such as astronomy. As well as pursuing his studies, Marlowe was embarking on a career as a writer. He translated Ovid's erotic *Elegies* from Latin into English, and Lucan's militaristic *Pharsalia*, and he probably wrote his first play, *Dido, Queen of Carthage*, while he was supposed to be preparing to enter the Church. In 1587, he took his MA and moved to London to write plays.

Radical dramatist

London was a place of tremendous excitement and opportunity for an aspiring playwright. Its population was nearly 200,000 and rising fast, and the professional theatre was just emerging, under the nominal patronage of people of influence, in converted inn yards and the first purpose-built theatres. The need to make money created pressure to find new material to attract audiences to come often. The government soon took advantage of this opportunity for mass dissemination of propaganda. There were no newspapers, and few could read books, so there was nothing to equal the power of the commercial theatre to reach out and communicate with the public. In 1583, the Queen had started to patronise her own troupe of actors, and the rhyming verse of the propaganda plays of the Queen's Men proved very popular. However, with the arrival of Thomas Kyd with *The Spanish Tragedy*, and then Christopher Marlowe with the two parts of *Tamburlaine the Great*, a revolution in the English theatre had begun and the two dramatists were overnight sensations.

With his cruel and implacable Scythian tyrant, Tamburlaine, Marlowe introduced a new kind of heroic **tragedy**, and the Admiral's Men had, in Edward Alleyn, an actor who rose to the part magnificently. The theatre rang with what Ben Jonson called Marlowe's 'mighty sounding rhyme'. It did not matter that most of the audience could not have understood the classical references, they sounded impressive, and it was the sound that captivated London audiences and that other dramatists sought to imitate. In this play, Marlowe turned away from the clumsy language and loose plotting of earlier dramatists and gave his audiences fresh vivid language, memorable action and intellectual complexity. Like the writers of classical tragedies, he focused on the inner turmoil of one man, rather than using his **protagonist** to represent mankind in general, as his precursors had done. He was not the first to use **blank verse** for his plays, but he was the first playwright to demonstrate the potential and versatility of blank verse as a dramatic medium. From now on, the Elizabethan audience would expect more than just entertainment. Thanks to Marlowe, they were looking for some serious exploration of ideas.

While Marlowe's fellow playwright, William Shakespeare, was beginning to explore English history, Marlowe deliberately chose controversial subjects for his plays. His central protagonists are often figures alienated from mainstream society.

As well as Tamburlaine, he based a play on Barabas, the Jew of Malta, who was not only a follower of a religion that was outlawed in England, but also a murderer and usurer. Dido, Queen of Carthage, was an African. Edward II was not only a weak king, but Marlowe also makes him overtly homosexual. *The Massacre at Paris* dealt with the massacre of Protestants by Catholics on Saint Bartholomew's Day, and in *Doctor Faustus* he was questioning the teaching of the Church itself.

Doctor Faustus

The first reference to Marlowe's *Doctor Faustus*, by William Prynne, was to a performance in Belsavage playhouse near St Paul's Cathedral, which was rarely used after 1588. It seems possible, therefore, that Marlowe may have written it soon after leaving Cambridge, while his expertise at theological arguments was fresh in his mind. Nevertheless, he was also immersed in the crowded theatre district of Shoreditch where he found lodgings. In using his low-life characters to explore the **themes** of the main **plot**, to re-enact it, to mock it and sometimes to predict it, Marlowe opened up new possibilities for English tragedy. The contrast between the dreadfully serious main plot and the crude, frivolous scenes with the clowns intensifies the trepidation but makes it more endurable because of the release of tension.

As in our own time, there was an appetite for sensation, and Marlowe provided it. Edward Alleyn, the leading actor of the Admiral's Men, the company for whom Marlowe was writing, wore a white surplice as Doctor Faustus, with a cross stitched on his breast to ward off the dangerous consequences of raising devils on stage. This provided a dramatic contrast to the delicious horror provided by the devils.

It was thought that the Devil actively seeks out solitary people who acknowledge no master. Faustus acknowledged no master until he signed a contract with Lucifer. If God has angels as messengers and a visible Church of believers, then it must have seemed logical that Satan must have demons as helpers and an invisible assembly of worshippers. The Church imagined the existence of an entire network of people who had sold their souls to Satan, worshipped him and dedicated their lives to harming and killing other people. To an Elizabethan audience, when a devil was invoked on stage, in a Latin incantation that only the most highly educated could understand, anything could happen!

Not surprisingly, the play was immensely popular, and this meant that it was frequently performed and often revised by acting companies. It was not published until 1604, more than ten years after the first recorded performance, so it is difficult to establish precisely what constituted the original play. Although it is fairly clear that Marlowe wrote the original script, combining slapstick and tragedy, without help, we know that Philip Henslowe paid William Birde and Samuel Rowley in 1602 for supplying additional text. The first edition of 1604 is now referred to as the A-text to distinguish it from the B-text, which appeared in 1616. It seems likely that Henslowe wanted more anti-papal feeling in the play, and the additions to the

second edition make Faustus more specifically an anti-Catholic hero. A rival German pope called Bruno is added as a foil to the Italian pope, and Faustus engages in more pranks, disguised as a cardinal. The A-text reflects the playwright's questioning attitude to religion and prioritises Faustus's inner turmoil, and so it seems more faithful to Marlowe's intention.

Violence and conspiracy

Life off stage was almost as explosive as the stories Marlowe depicted on stage. Gentlemen carried rapiers, and tempers were often short; a playgoer was once run through for arguing about the entrance fee. Spontaneous fights were frequent, and pre-arranged duels were fashionable. Shakespeare's *Romeo and Juliet* reflects the way young men would challenge each other to fights with rapiers over real or imagined slights. Usually these were merely excuses for displaying one's skill, courage and manliness, but occasionally someone died.

In 1589, Marlowe was drawn into a feud over an unpaid debt between his friend, Thomas Watson, and William Bradley, the son of an innkeeper. One afternoon, Marlowe and Bradley were duelling, obviously well-matched and enjoying the opportunity to show off their skills. However, Watson appeared and, since his quarrel was actually with Watson, Bradley turned to him and Marlowe withdrew. Watson was not as expert a fencer as his friend. He was hurt and, unable to fend off his opponent, he lunged and killed Bradley. Marlowe and Watson were arrested and sent to Newgate prison to await trial. After 13 days Marlowe was released, possibly through the intervention of the Privy Council to whom he was still useful as a courier. Watson was found to have killed in self-defence and was released later.

Whilst in Newgate, Marlowe met John Poole, who had been arrested for counterfeiting. Poole was related to Lord Strange, an important figurehead for those Roman Catholics who sought to replace Queen Elizabeth with a Catholic monarch. In 1592, Marlowe was arrested again in Flushing, now part of Holland, for counterfeiting coins with Richard Baines, a spy, and Gifford Gilbert, a goldsmith. The Catholic conspirators were financing their operations through theft and counterfeiting. Baines turned informant and accused Marlowe of working for the Catholic group which was plotting to kill Elizabeth. This may have been true, or, as he claimed, Marlowe might just have been keen to observe the goldsmith's skill. However, it could just have been need for money that motivated him, or perhaps he was trying to penetrate the Catholic plot to gain intelligence for the Privy Council. All we know for sure is that Marlowe was never punished and he was released soon afterwards.

Suppression of free speech

Once established as a poet and dramatist, Marlowe was able to mix with the greatest intellects of his age. Through the invitations of Henry Percy, Earl of Northumberland,

and of Sir Walter Raleigh, he would have met influential men like Dr John Dee, as well as other scientists and mathematicians who were questioning the Bible's accounts of such events as the Creation and the Fall. After the return of Drake's treasure-laden ship from its voyage round the world, Raleigh offered patronage to those whose knowledge and research might give England an advantage over its Catholic rival, Spain. In *Love's Labours Lost*, Shakespeare refers to this group of freethinkers as 'the School of Night', and in 1592, Robert Parsons initiated a widely read series of pamphlets accusing Raleigh and his associates of maintaining a 'schoole of Atheisme' led by a conjuror.

Accusations of atheism and witchcraft were a form of social control, designed to eliminate any form of social deviation, including those who voiced new ideas that were seen as subversive. It also served to demonstrate the power of the authorities and the danger of voicing unorthodox opinions. *Malleus Maleficarum* (literally 'the hammer of the wicked'), written in 1486 by two inquisitors of the Roman Catholic Church, became the manual for witch-hunters and inquisitors. The papal bull that prefaces this book states that witches were, first and foremost, arch-heretics.

Most of Marlowe's audience believed in witchcraft. During Elizabeth's reign there were 270 witch trials in England; however, the Queen was more lenient towards witches than her fellow monarchs in France and Spain. This may have been because her mother, Anne Boleyn, had been accused of witchcraft. Even in Protestant England, executions were conducted in such a way that the agony was prolonged for as long as possible so that both the victim and the spectators were given a glimpse of the everlasting torments associated with Hell. An execution was intended to warn people against questioning orthodox doctrine by representing not an end but a prelude to everlasting torture.

Marlowe was given a good understanding of the danger he was in when, in January 1589, Francis Kett, one of his university friends and a pious God-fearing man, was burned to death for denying the divinity of Christ. A witness described how Kett was lightly tied and went 'leaping and dancing: being in the fire, above twenty times' and 'clapping his hands he cried nothing but *blessed be God*', and so he continued 'until the fire had consumed all his nether parts, and until he was stifled with the smoke'. Marlowe knew what he was risking by voicing his doubts, but, in *Doctor Faustus*, he was careful to put anything that might be construed as subversive into the mouths of a devil or a man who was dragged to Hell in the end.

Plague

In the summer of 1592, the theatres in London were closed because of the plague, and Marlowe went home to Canterbury for a visit. The plague was an ever-present danger, giving everyone a feeling that their lives could be cut off at any time and enhancing their worry about what would happen after death. This fear meant that men like Chaucer's Pardoner did a brisk trade. This was a particularly virulent

outbreak during which some of Marlowe's friends and rivals died. There was a brief respite during an exceptionally cold winter, which killed many more, and then the plague returned in February 1593. This time the theatres remained closed for more than a year. Theatre companies went on the road, but evidence suggests that they had difficulty earning enough to cover their expenses. While theatre companies were not commissioning new plays, Marlowe needed to please his patron, Thomas Walsingham, and he turned once again to poetry, writing *Hero and Leander*.

Arrested again

Marlowe was staying with his patron in Kent in May when a placard was posted on a church wall in London, purporting to have been written by 'Tamburlaine'. At this time, Protestant refugees were fleeing to London to escape religious persecution on the Continent, and the placard advocated violence against these immigrants. He was arrested, taken to London and appeared before the Star Chamber, the powerful judicial arm of the Privy Council. His friend and fellow playwright, Thomas Kyd, had given evidence against him under torture, claiming that Marlowe had written a heretical treatise 'Denyinge the Deity of Jhesus Christ our Savior', and 'would report St John to be our Savior Christes Alexis [a boy loved by the shepherd Corydon in Virgil's *Eclogues*]…that is that Christ did love him with an extraordinary love.'

Marlowe was released on bail and Richard Baines was given the job of preparing the case against him. Marlowe had made an enemy of Baines while they were both working undercover in Flushing, and the other spy took his revenge. On 29 May, Baines presented to the Privy Council a long list of blasphemies and treasons that Marlowe is supposed to have said. He apparently averred 'that Christ was a bastard and his mother dishonest' and 'that St John the Evangelist was bedfellow to Christ and leaned always in his bosom, that he used him as the sinners of Sodoma'. Marlowe was accused not only of holding and uttering treasonable and atheistic opinions, but of persuading others, including some 'great men who in Convenient time shal be named', to the same beliefs. If the testimony is genuine, it is impossible to tell how much of his evidence revealed Marlowe's actual thoughts and how much was a result of his university training in playing devil's advocate in an argument.

Mysterious death

Marlowe was released on bail, and we can only conjecture what punishment awaited him, because on 30 May he was stabbed to death, not in an alehouse brawl as is often reported but in a respectable private dining house. The Coroner's report records that Marlowe, Ingram Frizer, a servant of Thomas Walsingham, and two former colleagues in Sir Francis Walsingham's secret service spent all day in discussions, sharing two meals. This suggests a business meeting rather than a drunken party and, more than 400 years later, there is still speculation that, instead of being

stabbed by Frizer in an argument over the bill, Marlowe was murdered to prevent him giving evidence against one or more of the 'great men' Baines links with him. Honan (2005) has unearthed evidence that Frizer was richly rewarded by Lady Audrey Walsingham, wife to Sir Thomas.

An alternative theory, explored in detail in *The Murder of the Man who was Shakespeare* by Calvin Hoffman, makes a quite convincing case for the proposal that Marlowe escaped to the Continent via the river and lived in exile, writing some of the plays that were attributed to Shakespeare. It is certainly strange that Marlowe, the most popular playwright of his time, is supposed to have been secretly buried in an unmarked grave.

The theatre

Medieval drama

In the Middle Ages, Christian ritual drama was staged to illustrate events of sacred history and the main doctrines of the Church. These **miracle plays** embraced the whole drama of humanity from the Creation of the World to the Last Judgement. Gradually, they moved outside the Church, where there was more space, more time and more freedom to entertain. Plays would be performed on wheeled drays that followed each other about the town in a pageant and eventually, these were taken over by the guilds, and each craft, or 'mystery', would have responsibility for a different part of the story. These were immense **epics** scenically presented rather than plays with plots and action. The Corpus Christi cycles, performed at Easter, became very elaborate affairs. Hell-mouth was portrayed as a monstrous face through which the souls of the damned would exit. On one occasion, the head of a stranded whale was used for this purpose, and two men worked the jaws as the actors ran in and out. Devils were very popular, providing that delicious horror which combines terror and hilarity, and they would descend from the cart to scare the crowd.

These plays were so popular that people did not just want drama at particular times of the year, so some of the stories were separated from the influence of the Church and became the subject of free dramatic handling. As well as biblical stories, ritualistic **morality plays** soon became very popular. They were allegoric dramas presenting the conflict of opposed powers for the soul of man. These dramas celebrate the truth of the Christian message, by showing stories of a protagonist called Mankind or Everyman who is tempted and transgresses, but repents and is redeemed. Unlike the pageants that travelled round the town, morality plays had to have a plot; the moral gave a point to which the action moved. Although they carried a serious message, they were nothing like a dry sermon; morality plays were colourful, comic, often **bawdy**, popular entertainment which attracted audiences

through a lively sense of fun. As in the 'mystery plays' the Vice character, who tempted the protagonist, was a clown, and the **Seven Deadly Sins** were played by comedians who indulged in irreverent horseplay and fooling.

Drama in the Elizabethan age

The popular drama Marlowe would have watched as he grew up was performed in fairgrounds, inn yards, noblemen's houses and arenas usually used for bull- or bear-baiting. People were accustomed to scenic representations, clumsy comedies and religious tragedies. By this time, as well as the biblical stories and the morality plays, political satires, romances, dramatised folk-tales and classical **myths** would all have helped to instil a love of theatre in the child. Marlowe, however, would also have become familiar with classical tragedies at school and university. When the influence of the Italian **Renaissance** reached England, the attention of educated people was directed to Latin and the Italian theatre, and they delighted in tragedies such as *Gorboduc*, which followed the model of Seneca, a Stoic philosopher from the first century AD. Marlowe would doubtless have been familiar with his plays in their original Greek, but, as part of the general revival that gives the Renaissance its name, Seneca's passionate revenge plays were translated into English in the second half of the sixteenth century.

Although early English plays provided some tragic material, particularly in some of the Bible stories, the great Renaissance tragedies of playwrights such as Marlowe and Shakespeare owed a significant debt to Seneca, although they put their own distinctive mark on the **genre**. The philosopher Aristotle said in his *Poetics* that tragedy is characterised by seriousness and dignity. It involves a great person who experiences a reversal of fortune, caused by a mistake of some kind that he made (*hamartia*). The **tragic hero** may achieve some revelation about or recognition of human fate, destiny and divine will (*anagnorisis*). Tragedy results in *catharsis* for the audience who feel emotionally cleansed after watching the suffering of the characters on stage. It is useful to bear this in mind in any discussion about whether *Doctor Faustus* is a tragedy or a morality play. The word 'tragedy' is derived from the Greek *tragoida* or 'goat-play', recognising that the tragic hero is a sacrifice to appease an angry god.

In the Middle Ages plays evolved from a number of scenes loosely linked together into a simple structure of temptation and weakening, followed by repentance and salvation. Thomas Kyd, Marlowe and others began to think more carefully about how to structure their plays, and they also experimented with **form**, eventually adopting blank verse as the most versatile medium for the stage. In Marlowe's *Doctor Faustus*, audiences were invited, for the first time on the English stage, to empathise with the tragic death of a man who had brought about his own downfall. It was not merely the mechanics of play writing, the language, structure and form, which were being revolutionised. An old-fashioned morality play shows the life and death of an allegorical protagonist to demonstrate how God's grace triumphs over the sins of the flesh, and the death of the reformed sinner is to be celebrated because he goes to Heaven. By contrast, a classical tragedy invites the audience to empathise with the dilemmas afflicting a particular individual who sets himself outside the established order of things, and to mourn his death. In *Doctor Faustus*, Marlowe blends the two traditions and exploits the tensions between them.

Patronage and independence

By the time Elizabeth came to the throne in 1558, there were professional companies of adult players and companies of boys drawn from choir schools. The companies were all licensed by the patronage of some person of influence to travel and perform, because unlicensed actors were regarded as vagabonds. Inevitably, the next step in the evolution of the English theatre was a permanent theatre, and in 1567, the Red Lion at Whitechapel was the first inn to be fitted with a stage and seats. The civic authorities of the City of London objected to the very idea of theatres on the grounds that they distracted people from their daily work and divine service on Sundays, and because they also encouraged crowds, which might lead to disorder and assist the spread of the plague. Permanent theatres were therefore built outside the city boundary, south of the Thames or to the north-east. *The Theatre* was erected in 1576 by James Burbage, a carpenter and entrepreneur, closely followed by *The Curtain* in 1577; another theatre was built in Newington a few years later, and *The Rose*, in 1587.

Unlike earlier actors, the new companies were financially dependent on a paying audience. They bore the name of a patron, but this was a legal requirement, and provided some measure of protection against interference by civic authorities and against political and religious censorship and suppression. Their patron would gain favour at court if their company pleased the Queen, and, of course, the company would gain prestige as well as money. In the theatres, the audience was drawn from a very wide range of social classes. The stage projected out into the audience, and apprentices and artisans could pay a penny to stand in the pit, while the more affluent could pay two pennies to sit in the galleries and could hire a cushion for another penny.

The opportunities offered by a permanent venue, the lack of elaborate scenery requiring clumsy scene changes, the disregarding of academic concerns of concepts such as the classical **unities** of time, place and action, all gave Renaissance playwrights in England the freedom to exercise their imaginations and those of their audiences. The influence of the Italian Renaissance liberated the spirit from authority and superstition; there were new approaches to the arts and sciences, new philosophical ideas, new political theories being explored. Simultaneously, the Reformation, which began in Germany, precipitated a revolt against the Roman Catholic Church as a dominant force and a new assertion of national independence

with the English monarch as the head of the Church in England. It was an age of innovation and exploration and no place was more inventive than the English stage.

English plays had evolved as the property of the people, not as texts to be studied by academics, so the most important consideration for the Elizabethan playwright was to sustain the interest of the audience and to excite their curiosity in what was to come. Elizabethan drama exercised the freedom of an island nation that had decisively detached itself from the Church in Rome when Henry VIII passed the Act of Supremacy in 1534, and whose Queen actively encouraged a spirit of nationhood, defiance against outside influence, supremacy over the waves and the exploration of the whole world. The theatre had the spontaneity of an art form of the people, and playwrights could exercise creative freedom, as long as they observed decorum in the elementary decencies of morals and religion.

Censorship

Puritans were vociferous in their condemnation of theatres, accusing them of promoting immorality of various kinds. Censorship was strictly imposed by the Lord Chamberlain via the Master of the Revels, a court officer in his service who had the pre-emptive right to censor plays and other public entertainments. It seems to have been erratic and unpredictable, but Queen Elizabeth forbade performance of all plays 'wherein either matters of religion or of the governance of the estate of the commonweal shall be handled or treated'. No atheistic, Catholic or even openly Puritan plays would have been allowed. Elizabeth was indignant about those who preached that there was no Hell but only a tormented conscience, so Marlowe was being prudent when he constructed his debate as a morality play and put such a heresy into the mouth of a devil, Mephistopheles. No other playwright dared to explore such issues.

The offence of blasphemy was punishable by fines, imprisonment and corporal punishment, and this was used as a legal instrument to persecute atheists, Unitarians and others whom the Lord Chamberlain wished to silence. The charge of blasphemy was brought against anyone who said or did anything that was considered to be irreverent towards God, Jesus Christ or the Holy Scriptures. When Marlowe was killed he was about to appear in court on the charge of holding 'blasphemous and damnable opinions'.

Permanent theatres

Elizabethan theatres were constructed to represent the universe. The canopies above the stage (where Faustus sees Christ's blood stream in the firmament) were called 'the heavens'; built into the stage was a trapdoor to the underworld from which devils could emerge and into which Faustus could be dragged at the end. Two columns supported the canopy and at the rear of the stage were two doors providing

entrances onto the stage, with an inner room sometimes between them. The companies created spectacles as brilliant and lavish as they could afford. Costumes were elaborate and often extravagant as they tried to create the illusion that the ordinary men in the company were kings, queens, cardinals or even the Pope. The players also made use of painted backdrops and a wide range of properties. The manager of the Admiral's Men, Philip Henslowe, kept meticulous records in which he writes of props such as tombs, a chariot, two steeples, several trees, a Hell-mouth and even 'the city of Rome' (presumably a painted curtain).

As in the inn yards, there was no roof, except over the seats and the stage, and performances took place in the afternoon, because there was no safe stage lighting. Theatres had wooden frames with plaster exteriors and the roofs were thatched, so there was constant danger of fire. The Globe Theatre went up in flames during a performance of Shakespeare's *Henry VIII* when a theatrical cannon misfired. Many different kinds of spectacular effects were created by the use of fireworks, trumpets, drums and guns to suggest battle scenes or storms, or to accompany devils. However, no attempt was made to create a stage location. The audiences were well used to using their imaginations and accepted whatever the actors told them. So, when Faustus is conjuring Mephistopheles in the middle of the night, it would not have been necessary to create literal darkness; Marlowe's poetry sets the scene admirably.

Play scripts

London doubled in population between 1580 and 1600 as its importance and wealth grew. The establishment of competing permanent theatres and professional companies created an inexhaustible demand for new material. Plays were performed every day, except during Lent or times of plague. The theatres could house an audience of between two and three thousand, so plays only ran for a few days and then audiences wanted something different; there was tremendous pressure on writers to produce something quickly. In Marlowe's day, texts of plays were not printed. A playwright would write for a company, not for publication. The versions that eventually found their way to the printing press would have been reconstructed from prompt copies of the scripts, including alterations by the directors, or from the memories of actors who spoke the lines, and, as a result, they are contaminated with errors and additions.

Doctor Faustus, for instance, may have been performed as early as 1588, although the first dated reference comes from 1594. The A-text, however, was not printed until 1604. A substantially different text was printed in 1616, now known as the B-text, and scholars are divided as to which text is closest to Marlowe's original. However, our task is to explore the play that has come down to us and not to speculate about the authorship of different scenes.

The Renaissance

The word 'Renaissance' comes from the French for 'rebirth', and it is used to identify a cultural movement which began in Italy (which had once been the home of the glorious Roman Empire) in the middle of the fourteenth century and spread to the rest of Europe by the sixteenth century. Dissatisfied with the teaching of the medieval Church, which concentrated on transcendental spirituality and frowned on attempts to understand the mysteries of God's creation, Renaissance thinkers scoured libraries in search of works by classical authors, typically written in Latin or ancient Greek, seeking to improve and perfect their worldly knowledge. Realism and the individual were at the centre of this movement. It was an exciting time of change and upheaval in almost every walk of life. There were significant changes in the way the universe was viewed and the methods with which philosophers sought to explain natural phenomena.

The new way of learning about the world focused on empirical evidence and direct observation, and this led to great contributions in the fields of astronomy, physics, biology and anatomy. Copernicus, for example, challenged scientific theory that the earth was stationary and at the centre of the universe; he proposed that it was instead the sun around which the earth and other planets revolved. Galileo (born in the same year as Marlowe and Shakespeare) proved Copernicus's helio-centric hypothesis with his telescope. Nevertheless, most educated Elizabethans still thought of the universe as geocentric, as it is described in the conversation between Faustus and Mephistopheles (2.3.35–64). Artists strove to portray the human form realistically, developing techniques to render perspective and light more naturally. Improvements in navigation and ship construction meant that adventurers could explore new worlds and bring back riches and stories of exotic foreign parts.

Writers were translating classical texts into vernacular languages and writing new works in the language of the common man. The invention of the printing press in the middle of the fifteenth century assisted the spread of the movement, making books more freely available and not so expensive. Because the Bible had been translated, ordinary people could read it and think for themselves, without being dependent on the priests to interpret the word of God. By the time Marlowe was writing, Puritans were beginning to advocate a belief in individual obedience to the dictates of one's own conscience, a view that was seen as subversive because it threatened the power and authority of the Church.

The Great Chain of Being

The Church clung to the classical theory of the Great Chain of Being that was presumed to stretch from the foot of God's throne down to the meanest of objects. At the bottom of the chain is the inanimate class of things, the elements, liquids and metals, which have existence but no life. Next comes the vegetative class of things

that have existence and life, followed by those creatures that have existence, life and feeling. Above these come human beings who have existence, life, feeling and understanding, and so sum up the total faculties of earthly phenomena. (For this reason man is often described in literature as a little world or microcosm.) Above human beings are angels who are purely spiritual but are linked to people by under-standing, although angels have intuitive understanding while people have to strive for it. Above angels is God, who is absolute perfection.

Within each class there is another strict hierarchy, and therefore everybody in the human race has another person above and below. Although what sets human beings apart from animals is their capacity for reason, it was thought that they should use their capacity for reasoning to study to know themselves and to learn about God, not to fathom the secrets of the universe and not to strive to improve their ranking. People have been given free will, but it was thought that the right use of that will was to bend our souls towards having and doing only that which we perceive to be morally good. If people study to lift themselves above their allotted position, as Faustus does, this will break a link in the chain and lead to disorder.

Renaissance man

The term 'Renaissance man' is frequently used to describe a polymath, or a well-educated person whose knowledge is not restricted to one subject area. In Renaissance Italy, a highly respected polymath, Leon Battista Alberti (1404–72), was the first to assert that 'a man can do all things if he will', and this statement developed into the notion that people should embrace knowledge in all fields and stretch their capacities as fully as possible. Alberti himself was an architect, painter, poet, scientist, mathematician, inventor and sculptor, as well as a skilled horseman and archer. Nicolaus Copernicus was also a true Renaissance man; as well as an astronomer, he was a lawyer, tax-collector, doctor, military governor, judge and vicar-general of canon law. Military commanders, like Sir Philip Sidney and Sir Walter Raleigh, were poets as well.

The Renaissance period spanned roughly the fourteenth to the seventeenth centuries, and at this time universities did not specialise in specific areas as they do today, but rather trained their students in a broad spectrum of science, philosophy and theology. As the play opens, Doctor Faustus has already excelled at Divinity, Logic, Medicine and the Law, and is looking for something more challenging which will bring him 'a world of profit and delight, / Of power, of honour, of omnipo-tence' (1.1.55–56). Above all, he seeks knowledge; he wants spirits to 'Resolve (him) of all ambiguities' (1.1.82) and explain to him all the mysteries of the world.

Leonardo da Vinci

It is interesting to compare Marlowe's fictional character with real-life Renaissance men such as Leonardo da Vinci (1452–1519). Da Vinci was not only a painter and

sculptor, but also an engineer, astronomer, anatomist, biologist, geologist, physicist, architect, philosopher and, of course, inventor. He wanted to fly and invented different kinds of flying machines; he wanted to create life and invented a robot; he drew detailed diagrams of a host of other inventions that would enable man to overcome nature. He studied everything around him and concluded that the Bible was wrong in saying that the world was created in seven days because he found evidence that it had evolved over many centuries. Da Vinci explored the bodies of the dead to find out how the body worked; his contemporaries were outraged and he was accused of heresy and necromancy. A **metaphorical** way of describing da Vinci's deliberate flouting of the Church would be to say that he had sold his soul, his hope of Heaven, in return for knowledge.

Many Renaissance thinkers based their researches on Natural Laws of God. They argued that, over time, civilisation had gradually suppressed the conscious collective memory or history of natural laws that had come down through the generations. They were convinced that they had a responsibility to work to help bring people back to God, because they had been cut off by the instituted supremacy of the governing laws of society and the oppression of the Church. The primary rule of nature was perceived as mankind's direct relationship with God. These men and women felt that, by helping each individual to reach high within themselves for direct, inner knowledge from God, they would be assisting in the spiritual evolution of the whole of mankind, and evil persecution in the world would naturally come to an end.

Dr John Dee

Dr John Dee was one such man. He believed it was his sacred duty to harness the occult forces of the universe for the benefit of mankind. In 1564, Dee wrote a treatise called *Monas Hieroglyphica*, in which he dealt with mankind's spiritual transformation and the need to return to our original divine nature. Dee believed that the divine essence, a part of God in every man and woman, was an aspect of humankind that had been lost or forgotten and must be rediscovered. A very devout man, Dee saw mathematics as the key to all knowledge at a time when maths was considered to be a branch of black magic, involving the use of arcane **symbols** in attempts to understand and control the natural world.

Some historians suggest that Dee played a major role in laying the foundations for the Age of Enlightenment. He wrote a number of influential books, including ones on mathematics, geometry, navigation, geography, astronomy, philosophy and chemistry. His *Mathematical Preface to Euclide's Geometry* (1570) was the first treatise in history that was specifically directed to scientists, and it was written in English instead of Latin in order to open the world of science to each individual. He was responsible for major advances in navigation, and it was he who proposed the programme of explorations to discover new lands. He was court astrologer and confidant to Elizabeth I, who used to visit him at his home in Mortlake, where he had the largest library in England. His plan was to create a national library, and he collected about 4,000 manuscripts of some of the world's most significant classical writings. Unfortunately, after he left for the Continent in 1583, a mob sacked his library, plundering and destroying his books and scientific instruments.

On 22 December 1581, with his assistant Edward Kelly, Dr John Dee reportedly began to summon spirits and interrogate them about the nature of the universe. He kept careful records of the conversations they had with angels both good and evil. It is generally accepted now that Kelly was a very clever confidence trickster who persuaded Dee that he could interpret messages from the spirit world, and who represented himself as the channel through which the spirits would speak. However, his trickery depended on the fact that Elizabethans believed in spirits. It was not contradictory for a man of science to seek to improve his knowledge this way, because the dividing lines between alchemy and chemistry, between astrology and astronomy, between magic and science, were not as clear-cut as they are today. Without an understanding of the law of gravity, it is perhaps rational to explain the way in which snowflakes fall to earth by saying that spirits carry them. Without an understanding of bacteria, it is not surprising that people blamed witchcraft for sudden, unexplained illness.

Christopher Marlowe almost certainly met Dee, who was also one of those intellectuals Raleigh gathered around him who were dubbed the 'School of Night'. It is reasonable to assume then that Marlowe knew of Dee's occult researches, and, although Doctor Faustus is not based directly on Dr Dee, knowledge of the latter definitely illuminates our understanding of Marlowe's protagonist. Doctor Faustus also simultaneously displays intellectual brilliance, the admirable Renaissance spirit of aspiration and determination to push beyond human limitations, as well as the mental obtuseness which made him vulnerable to the dubious study of magic and the conjuring of spirits.

Renaissance magic

> *Magick Art* (magia) in general, is wisdom or contemplation of heavenly
> Sciences, and is two fold; Natural, which is lawful, and is the ground of all true
> Physick, and the occult wisdom of nature, without which all mans Reason and
> Knowledge is Ignorance; The other is Diabolical, superstitious and unlawful,
> and is called Necromancy: whereby men attain to the knowledge of things by
> the assistance of evil spirits.
> Thomas Blount, *Glossographia* (1656)

Magicians in the Hermetic and Paracelsan traditions, followers of Cornelius Agrippa and Paracelsus, asserted that 'natural' magic was the first stage of an aspiration to divine wisdom. They asserted that their knowledge and abilities were derived from

God, and that people, being partly divine, were capable of controlling those below them in the Great Chain of Being.

They believed civilisation was on the brink of a renewal of knowledge that would restore to men the powers originally given us by God, when he gave man 'dominion over the fish of the sea, and over the fowl of the air, and over the cattle, and over all the earth, and over every creeping thing that creepeth upon the earth' (Genesis 1:26). They argued that the innocence lost when Adam and Eve fell from grace can be repaired by religion and faith, and that our dominion over creation could, at least in part, be restored through the study of natural science. They predicted that this renewal of man's knowledge would bring with it the reform of society and even human nature itself.

Black and white magic

Magicians believed that magical power was derived from the magus's ability to purify the soul and so return it to its condition before the Fall. The magus can attain a godlike status through the reflection of the entire cosmos within his own soul; the mind becomes all things and, in doing so, it becomes one with God. Devout philosophers, such as John Dee and Giordano Bruno, attempted to distinguish between their own intellectual magic and Satanic witchcraft or common superstition. They made a distinction between benevolent 'white' magic, which sought to control the elements through natural philosophy and supernatural wisdom, and malevolent 'black' magic.

Black magic draws on malevolent powers; it involves having dealings with the Devil and conjuring up the dead through necromancy. It may be used for dark purposes or vicious acts that deliberately cause harm to others. Both black and white magic are forms of sorcery, but they are ideologically and morally opposed. In Tolkien's *The Lord of the Rings*, the elves find it strange that humans and hobbits can use a single word, 'magic', which refers to both — since in the Elvish tongues they are regarded as completely separate and unrelated.

In the sixteenth century, those who practised white magic were devout Christians. In *De occulta philosophia* (1531), Agrippa warns the prospective magus to 'implore God the Father…that you may be worthy of His mercy'. He claimed: 'Nothing is concealed from the wise and sensible, while the unbelieving and unworthy cannot learn the secrets.' Paracelsus insisted that the search for occult virtues should proceed through practical experience, guided and illuminated by God. Alchemists believed that, under the correct astrological conditions, base metals such as lead could be 'perfected' into gold. They tried to hasten this process by heating and refining the metal in a variety of chemical processes, most of which were kept secret.

Paracelsus believed that alchemy was redemptive, that it was a power given to man so that we can improve our condition after the Fall: 'Many have said of

Alchemy, that it is for the making of gold and silver. For me such is not the aim, but to consider only what virtue and power may lie in medicines.' Another of the alchemists' goals was to create the elixir of life, a remedy that, supposedly, would cure all diseases and prolong life indefinitely. Alchemy symbolised evolution from an imperfect, corruptible and ephemeral state towards a healthy, incorruptible and everlasting state. Paracelsus also asserted that God intended the wise to gradually perfect their knowledge so that eventually they could overthrow the ignorant who opposed them.

Dreams of empire

At the time Marlowe was writing, Francis Drake had recently returned from his circumnavigation of the globe, so Englishmen began to dream of an English empire that would rival that of the Spaniards in wealth and power. After the defeat of the Armada in 1588, the dream became tangible, and aspirations for wealth, military success and political glory encouraged the study of sciences that would give man control over the **elements**. The growing scientific community in London was stimulating renewed interest in investigating alchemy. Philosophers and scientists believed that religion was about to be freed from superstition, that the arts and the sciences would dominate and that full control over our environment was within our grasp.

Witchcraft

However, some of these new explorations led intellectuals into conflict with the Church. The authorities in the Church and in the state certainly did not want there to be reform in society. A belief that one possessed occult wisdom was seen by the orthodox as an illusion born of excessive pride, and there was a widespread fear that a quest for knowledge about the universe would result in revolutions in religion, politics and other spheres. Orthodox treatises condemned all magic as witchcraft, and accusations of witchcraft and atheism were used to suppress freedom of enquiry. The papal bull that prefaces the inquisitors' manual, *Malleus Maleficarum*, reminded them that witches were arch-heretics. The persecution of witches was a reaction against the progressive and revolutionary forces that were associated with the occult tradition.

William Perkins, Marlowe's professor of theology at Cambridge and part of the establishment, taught that Satan's kingdom was upheld by witches who fall prey to two major categories of temptation. First, there are those who are unwilling to accept their subordinate social status and who wish to use their magical powers to attain wealth and political power; second, there are those who are dissatisfied with the limitations of the human mind and who feel an excessive thirst for knowledge. He argued that magicians derive whatever powers they possess from the superior scientific knowledge of the Devil, who may enable his followers to perform certain

feats in order to win himself a following among the gullible. Marlowe clearly draws on this teaching in his portrayal of Doctor Faustus.

Marlowe's play shows how debates about religion began to be openly discussed, even in the theatre. To create drama, he draws on the conflict between this conventional theological teaching and the debates among free-thinking intellectuals. One of the central conflicts of *Doctor Faustus* is whether magic and the vision of the limitless extent of human potential that it offers are illusions, or whether it is traditional orthodoxy that deals with illusions. Magic in *Doctor Faustus* is a unifying symbol that draws together three aspects of Renaissance thought that had already been justified by occult philosophers. People's love of earthly beauty was seen to spring from our visionary powers and our love of God. Both political ambition and the pursuit of infinite knowledge were explained as resulting from the awareness of the immortality and divinity of the human soul.

Through his use of magic, Marlowe focuses on the central question of the limits of human nature, but he maintains a calculated **ambivalence**, giving voice to some of the issues being debated but putting them in the mouths of a devil or a man who is eventually damned. *Doctor Faustus*, Marlowe's contribution to the debate, suggests that, because people are beings in whom good and evil are intermingled, the process of purification that the magicians described is impossible. The aspiration to attain a godlike status and to exert benevolent control over society is almost inevitably corrupted by selfish desires for wealth, sensual indulgence, and political power.

The Tempest

More than 20 years later, Shakespeare also explored magic as a theme in his final play, *The Tempest*. In claiming that his 'secret studies' are devoted to the 'bettering of my mind', Prospero casts himself as a benevolent magician, in contrast with Sycorax whom he claimed was diabolical, making 'earthy and abhorred commands'. As Paracelsus advised, Prospero has been gradually perfecting his knowledge so that he can overthrow his enemies. Through years of study, contemplation and reflection upon his experience, Prospero has apparently brought his own soul into harmony with the cosmic order, and consequently his art is presented as a means through which God's will is accomplished.

However, like Marlowe, Shakespeare also suggests that the magicians' vision of universal harmony will never be perfectly realised in this world. Through his magic, Prospero apparently strives to bring about the harmonious union between the natural and supernatural dimensions of reality, symbolised by the marriage of Earth and Heaven in the masque he conjures. Significantly, however, the masque is interrupted when Prospero is 'distempered' with anger. It was believed that violent 'passion' derived from imbalance between the four **humours** (black bile, phlegm, blood, yellow bile), so, like Faustus, Prospero is a man with human weaknesses. He has not yet liberated his soul from his own passions and achieved

perfect spiritual harmony. At the end of the play, he is forced to accept the limitations of the power of good over evil when he says of Caliban: 'this thing of darkness I acknowledge mine'.

Prospero and Faustus both seem to blur the distinction between black and white magic. Just as Faustus derives his magical powers from Mephistopheles, Prospero achieves his magical effects through Ariel, a spirit of the air, whom he describes as a 'malignant thing' (1.2.257), possibly because he is angry, but he could be suggesting that Ariel is not a divine agent. Prospero knows that he should achieve control over his passions and strives to achieve it: 'Though with their high wrongs I am struck to th' quick, / Yet with my nobler reason 'gainst my fury/ Do I take part' (5.1.25–27). However, immediately after this, he claims that 'Graves at my command/ Have wak'd their sleepers, op'd, and let 'em forth/ By my so potent art' (5.1.48–50). Although some Renaissance texts asserted that there are means of raising the dead which derive directly from God and that are consequently classed as miracles, there is nothing to suggest that Prospero was acting benevolently.

Shakespeare uses the term 'rough magic' to refer to this and other destructive acts that Prospero boasts of, such as setting 'roaring war' between the sea and sky, and splitting 'Jove's stout oak/ With his own bolt'. In the same speech, Prospero renounces his magic. He has achieved the necessary control over nature and over himself, and he has no more need of the means by which he achieved it. Perhaps Shakespeare is suggesting that, because magicians inevitably suffer from human weaknesses, they will never be able to purify their souls, and Prospero has achieved enough self-knowledge to realise that he can go no further towards achieving the godlike status Renaissance magicians aspired to. Both Marlowe and Shakespeare communicate the aspirations of these men of vision, but keep the audience aware of their mortality.

The Faust legend

The Bible (in Apostles 8:9–13, 18–24) tells of a magician called Simon who convinced the people that he was 'the great power of God' because 'he had bewitched them with his sorceries'. In the folklore of nearly all countries there are stories about people who have made 'a bond with iniquity', but the **legend** of a man who makes an actual contract with the Devil seems to have first appeared in the sixth century with the legend of St Theophilus who, having lost his post as bishop, signed a blood pact with Satan in order to regain it; Theophilus, however, repented. In the tenth century, a nun, Hrosvitha of Gandersheim, used the story for a play, written in Latin. This play was translated into all the major European languages, and in the fifteenth century it was included among the lives of the saints in Jacobus de Voragine's *Golden Legend*, printed by William Caxton.

The man behind the myth

In the early sixteenth century, the legend became identified with a Doctor Faust or Faustus who was born around 1480 in Kündlingen, in Germany. He graduated from Heidelberg University in 1509, coming first in a group of 16 students of Philosophy. He was reported to be the friend of Paracelsus and Cornelius Agrippa, two erudite men who are chiefly remembered for their experiments in the occult arts, as well as of the Lutheran reformer Franz von Sickingen, one of the greatest patrons of literature and learning of his time.

There are records of some of the predictions that earned Faustus his reputation. He was paid ten guilders (a very large sum, enough to buy a horse) for having drawn up the horoscope of the Bishop of Bamberg. In 1535, the *Waldeck Chronicle* records that he had correctly prophesied that the city of Münster would be captured. In 1540, Philipp von Hutten wrote to his brother that he 'must confess that the philosopher Faust hit the nail on the head' in prophesying 'a very bad year', whereas the famous philologist Camerarius had consistently predicted success. However, even before Faustus left university, he was gaining a reputation as a boaster and black magician. In 1507, Johann Trittheim, a Benedictine abbot in Würzburg, tutor of Cornelius Agrippa, and a learned writer on occultism and demonology, wrote to a friend that: 'The man of whom you wrote me, who has presumed to call himself the prince of necromancers, is a vagabond, a babbler and a rogue.' He claims that he heard Doctor Faustus boast that, if all the works of Plato and Aristotle were burned, he could restore them from memory.

There is a story that Faust was able to treat all his friends in a tavern to endless drinks by drilling holes in the table and causing wine to bubble up through them. Another story says that he threatened a clergyman by vowing that he could cause all the pots in the kitchen to fly up through the chimney. In 1532, the city council of Nuremberg denied safe conduct to 'Doctor Faust, the great sodomite and necromancer'. Like a fairground charlatan, he arrogantly advertised himself as 'fountain of necromancers, astrologer, *magus secundus*, chiromancer, aeromancer, pyromancer, second in hydromancy'. However, he was not actually linked with the Devil until Martin Luther, speaking in 1537 about 'magicians and the magic art and how Satan blinded men', claimed that Faustus called the Devil his 'brother-in-law'.

Faustus was killed in 1540 or 1541 when his chemicals suddenly exploded during an experiment. In 1548, Johannes Gast, a Protestant clergyman of Basel, described his death in this way: 'the wretch was destined to come to a deplorable end, for he was strangled by the devil and his body on its bier kept turning face downward even though it was five times turned on its back. God preserve us lest we become slaves of the devil'. It seems that he died while seeking to satisfy his intellectual curiosity; his motto could be the one on the portrait believed to be of Marlowe: *quod me nutrit me destruit*, 'that which nourishes me destroys me'.

The Faust legends are to be found in a number of books and ballads, the first of which to be published was the *Historia von D. Johan Faustens*, published in Germany in 1587 and known as the *Faustbuch*. This book pretended to be an authentic biography, but it is almost entirely fictional. Very little of this was invented by its anonymous author, who drew on the legends which had grown up around the man; however, one important addition was that, in order to create the feel of a biography, both Faustus and the Devil had to be given characters. Until the *Faustbuch*, diabolical familiars had rarely been made characters or even given names, and the name of Mephistopheles seems to have been newly coined by the author. The most likely derivation is from the Greek *mephotophiles* meaning 'no friend to light' in a **parody** of the name Lucifer, meaning 'light-bearer' in Latin. Alternatively, it might have come from a Hebrew word meaning 'destroyer of the good' or from two Hebrew words meaning 'liar' and 'destroyer'.

Marlowe's adaptation

We know that by 1592 the *Faustbuch* had been translated into English, and Marlowe follows this translation very closely. However, instead of a disapproving voice telling the story of Faustus, the wandering magician who sought worldly pleasures, Marlowe explores the psychology of a man who desires the infinite, a man who understands the risks he is taking but throws caution to the winds in his pursuit of intellectual power. Marlowe gives Faustus the aspiration for 'a world of profit and delight,/ Of power, of honour, of omnipotence'. By contrast, in the translation, the pact with the Devil is made because Faust exhibits a wicked pride and is not content with 'that vocation whereunto it hath pleased God' to call him. Being, like Marlowe, 'base of stock' but university educated, Marlowe's protagonist rejected the medieval idea that it was the individual's religious and moral duty to remain within his assigned place in the social hierarchy.

Unlike his model, Marlowe's Faustus seems disappointed with his bargain from the start. He repeatedly thinks of repentance and the only experience he seems to regard as wholly living up to his expectations is the appearance of Helen. In the translation of the *Faustbuch* there is a detailed description of Helen as she looks around her 'with a roling hawke's eye'. She becomes the 'common concubine and bed-fellow' of Faustus and has a child called Justus Faustus who, together with his mother, vanishes after Faustus's death. Marlowe clearly wants to lift Helen above the fact that on stage she is in reality a boy dressed in a woman's clothes. He leaves Helen's beauty to the audience's imagination, relying on Faustus's eloquence as he imagines what she will inspire him to do and how much fairer she is than the most beautiful characters in classical mythology.

Like an alchemist, Marlowe took the base metal of the *Faustbuch* and turned it into gold with his magnificent poetry. He created the potential for memorable drama when he added stage directions with devils and fireworks, the Good and Evil

Angels, and the Seven Deadly Sins. Marlowe concentrated on the internal struggle of his protagonist, omitting many of the petty instances of Faust's abuse of his magical powers and much of the moralising by the narrator. He was the first to arouse compassion for a man who makes a pact with Satan, but he was not the last writer to adapt the legend to his own time. The Faust story, in a variety of guises, was retold in Europe throughout the eighteenth and nineteenth centuries, most famously by Goethe at the beginning of the nineteenth century.

Free will

The story of the Faustian pact explores the concept of free will — whether and in what sense people exercise control over their actions and decisions. According to the doctrine of free will, our choices are not forced, as the path of a river is forced by its channel, but we are free to go in what direction we choose. In a religious context, God has given people free will so that we can make the choice for ourselves to obey Him, and, if our faith is strong, like that of the Old Man in *Doctor Faustus*, evil cannot harm us. The Old Man views the actions of the devils as a test of his faith, imposed by God, like the Tree of Knowledge in the Garden of Eden.

The powers of evil can do nothing unless people succumb to temptation. Mephistopheles cannot approach Faustus until the scholar blasphemes, just as Chaucer's fiend cannot suggest poison to the youngest rioter in *The Pardoner's Tale* until he wishes to have the gold all to himself. The witches only approach Macbeth because he already has 'black and deep desires'. At any time, Faustus could choose to repent; according to free will, the future is not decided until the moment that it arrives in the present. Even in our rational and scientific age, writers are intrigued by the paradox that God has given people curiosity and aspiration, but then He punishes us for following these driving forces. He has given us appetites and desires which He has declared it sinful to pursue. He says we have free will, but He knows in advance what our choices will be.

Later adaptations

Early in the nineteenth century, Johann Wolfgang von Goethe wrote a much more complex version of the legend. His Faust is favoured by God for his quest for the true essence of life. However, frustrated with learning and the limits to his knowledge and power, he attracts the attention of Mephistopheles, who has a wager with God that he can tempt Faust away from God and thereby win his soul for all eternity.

One twentieth-century novelist who reworked the Faust legend was Thomas Mann. His novel, *Doktor Faustus* (1947), is set during the first half of the twentieth century. The hero, a fictional German composer named Adrian Leverkühn (meaning 'living audaciously'), displayed uncommon brilliance as a musician in his youth, and this led to a personal career and life-drama in which he is increasingly preoccupied with the judgement of his soul.

The film *The Devil's Advocate* (1997) is a more recent reworking of the legend, involving a young provincial lawyer who successfully defends a man he knows to be guilty, sacrificing everything he holds dear because of his ambition. Later, when he does express moral misgivings, the choice is left up to him. Like Marlowe's Mephistopheles, his tempter does not persuade him but offers to take him off the case. The lawyer ends up in his own hell, because he has only himself to blame for everything that happens.

The play on stage

The first recorded performance of *Doctor Faustus* was in 1594, but it had almost certainly been produced before then. It was an immediate box office hit, and Philip Henslowe records exceptionally high takings from its performances. However, its content engendered severe criticism from Puritans such as Prynne who wrote of 'the visible apparition of the Devill on the stage at the Belsavage Play-house, in Queene Elizabeths days, (to the great amazement both of the Actors and Spectators) whiles they were there prophanely playing the History of Faustus'.

The terrifying nature of its subject gave rise to other such tales. At one performance the theatre is said to have 'cracked' and frightened the audience; at another, actors were reported to have become convinced that there was an extra devil on stage: 'Certaine Players at Exeter acting upon the stage the tragical storie of Dr Faustus the conjurer; as a certain nomber of Devells kept everie one his circle there, and as Faustus was busie in his magicall invocations, on a sudden they were all dasht, every one harkning other in the eare, for they were all perswaded there was one devell too many amongst them.' The audience fled and the actors are reported to have spent the night in reading and prayer.

Stories such as these must have acted as an excellent advertisement for a play that provided the delicious horror that audiences have always loved. Certainly the stage effects provided a talking point. In 1620, John Melton wrote of a performance at the Fortune Theatre where 'a man may behold shagge-hayr'd Deuills runne roaring over the Stage with Squibs in their mouthes, while Drummers make Thunder in the Tyring-house, and the twelue-penny Hirelings make artificiall Lightning in their Heavens'. Parliament closed the theatres in England in 1642, six years before the execution of Charles I, and they did not open again until the return of Charles II. In 1662, Samuel Pepys watched *Doctor Faustus* at the Red Bull theatre and declared the play 'so wretchedly and poorly done, that we were sick of it'. Certainly it is a play which depends very much for its success on the staging.

Seventeenth and eighteenth centuries

During the next two centuries, *Doctor Faustus* was performed only as pantomime or puppet shows, although the play was very popular on the Continent, especially

in Germany. The next serious production in England was produced by William Poel for the Elizabethan Stage Society in 1896. He staged the play as he thought it would have been performed for the Elizabethans, even introducing a hell's mouth at the end. Faustus himself was portrayed as an aspiring Renaissance scholar, bravely risking everything for knowledge of the universe.

Early twentieth century

Early twentieth-century productions similarly offered a romantic view of the hero. Most modern productions draw on both the A- and the B-texts to support their interests and interpretations. In 1937 there was a memorable production by John Housman and Orson Welles, who played the title role. Welles believed in the Devil and magic so he associated himself with the doomed genius and gave an intensely personal performance. Welles was a keen amateur magician, so he used the tricks of the trade to delight audiences with the special effects. The scene at the papal court had a black velvet background and actors dressed in black so that lighting could be used to create the appropriate illusions. There was a procession of sumptuous dishes for the Pope's feast, which came to a halt as a suckling pig and other animals rose into the air and danced, recalling Prospero's demonstration of power and contempt for the gluttony of his victims. Ceremonial headdresses were whisked off by wires, and a flash box exploded under the Pope's robes accompanied by cries of terror and fiendish laughter. The procession broke up leaving Faustus suddenly alone on an empty stage.

OUDS production, 1966

The first production to break with the traditional portrayal of the aspiring romantic was Nevill Coghill's 1966 Oxford University Dramatic Society production starring Richard Burton and Elizabeth Taylor. Coghill saw *Doctor Faustus* as a morality play with an ordinary man as the hero, a man who was a brilliant scholar but who also had basic human needs and appetites. Andreas Teuber, the American student who was given the role of Mephistopheles, has spoken and written about the stage production and the film that was made later. The film set was designed 'to resemble the interior of a man's skull, each vaulted corner another cavity of his mind. As the camera moves from the bookshelves, filled with tomes on history, religion and law, through the elaborate maze of chemistry apparatus, to the crucifix, it is meant to be exploring Faustus' mind, not just his room.'

Teuber portrayed Mephistopheles as a 'waiting, watching devil' who knew from first-hand experience what Faustus would be giving up if he signed the contract. He 'cannot quite believe what he is hearing from Faustus, that he's so ready, so willing to give up his soul.' He could not say too much, however, because Lucifer was watching him, so Teuber turned away and did not look directly at Faustus. He revealed his feelings through his hands, the way he stood and through the tear he shed when Faustus started to talk to Mephistopheles about coming to his study and consummating the sale of his soul. He shed another tear at the very end, as Faustus descended into Hell. Teuber says: 'Mephistopheles is not a tempting devil. He's just a messenger; the salesman "on the floor", so to speak. Events unfold around him, but he himself does very little.'

Teuber feels that Mephistopheles is 'pulling for Faustus', that Marlowe wanted to create dramatic tension by leaving open the possibility that Faustus might repent right up to the very end. 'I do believe that Marlowe wrote each scene with the thought at the back of his mind: perhaps in this scene Faustus will repent…What better way to bring this possibility home than to have Mephistopheles play little or no role in Faustus' damnation, than to keep the focus on Faustus, than to let Faustus be master of his own fate?' He adds: 'Mephistopheles does not trip Faustus up; Faustus trips over his own two feet. He does not tempt Faustus; Faustus tempts himself and Mephistopheles watches and waits. Therein lies the genius of the play.'

Recent productions

By contrast, Adrian Noble's production at the Royal Exchange, Manchester, in 1981, used Mephistopheles to integrate the comic scenes with the main plot. He turned the pages of the book for Robin as he had done for Faustus, helped with the pronunciation of 'Demogorgon' and whispered in Rafe's ear.

John Barton's 1974 touring production for the Royal Shakespeare Company marginalised Mephistopheles, focusing on the hero's mental anguish. Ian McKellen played Faustus as an intensely intellectual and dispirited hero. The play was set entirely in Faustus's book-lined study which was designed to suggest the interior of a skull, and the comic scenes were omitted. Puppets operated and voiced by Faustus were used for the Sins, the Angels and also for Helen, suggesting that everything was occurring in Faustus's own mind. However, devils spoke the Chorus's lines, suggesting that Lucifer was controlling everything that happened.

David Lan's 2002 production for the Young Vic also offered an intense psychological interpretation of Faustus. The critic Benedict Nightingale wrote that Jude Law 'catches that central contradiction of his period: that curiosity is a need and joy but also a danger and destroyer'. Mephistopheles, played by Richard McCabe, was 'a quiet, grave demon who momentarily, agonisingly returns to sentient life when he recalls his own damnation, but otherwise exudes the awful fatalism of someone who has dug his own grave and kept climbing downwards'. Nightingale concludes: 'In an age of unbelief, [the cast] generate the intensity to hold us rapt through an Elizabethan play about the lure of Lucifer.'

David Lan spoke in a interview about how he thinks the play can speak to an audience today: 'It is a play about people trying to work out what it is to be a human being, given that people are consumed by powerful urges, needs and

desires which they don't often entirely understand – either why they want what they want or exactly what it is that they want. But as we know, hungers of various kinds can completely take over and sometimes destroy people's lives, and the play is very fascinatingly practical about those forces in people's lives. It shows people deliberately trying to understand life and the world around them. Trying to work out what it is, trying to get mastery over it and trying to take control of what happens to them.'

In 2004, there was an exciting ensemble promenade production in Chichester, which involved local people as well as professional actors. The play opened in the theatre, but then the audience was guided down North Street, past various scenes of the play, to the impressive medieval cathedral for a most dramatic finale. The theatre's dramaturge, Edward Kemp, wrote: 'The many locations and diverse acting experience of the performers force the production to run the full gamut from austere contemporary classicism in the Minerva to medieval declamation in the Cathedral (how else can one be heard?) by way of pageant, art installation, street theatre and promenade.'

Shenandoah Shakespeare

There was an interesting American production in 2000 by Shenandoah Shakespeare, directed by Ralph Alan Cohen. Cohen 'wanted people to be ravished by the aspirations of Faustus, to like him because he is so curious, because the universe for him is so full of possibility, and because possibility is so alluring — "all things that move between the quiet poles shall be at my command"'. He also wanted to show Faustus's courage in seeking to terrify us. He wanted the audience to ask: 'How can Faustus be stupid, smart, and sympathetic simultaneously?' Cohen used the B-text and explained: 'In my view, Faustus is Disintegrating Man. Once he cuts himself off from God, the mathematics of the play is subtraction. First he cannot be two (he cannot marry, and therefore is reduced to a sterile, un-reproducing one). Then he loses his head. Then he loses his limbs. Then he is torn to pieces. Even the poetry of his final speech is all about his being atomised.'

Perhaps the most interesting feature of the production was that Cohen cast the same actress as Mephistopheles and Helen. 'I wanted a Mephistopheles that was chilling AND seductive…who might really have been one of God's most beautiful angels…who was curious about Faustus, delighted with having a smart opponent, and envious that such an opponent could turn back, if he chose to.' When Chaon Cross removed the friar's hood she wore as Mephistopheles to reveal that she was also Helen of Troy, many in the audience apparently gasped in amazement.

Productions can give totally opposing interpretations because there are two texts from which directors can cherry-pick scenes and lines to support their views. Faustus can be portrayed as a romantic figure with overwhelming aspirations, a tortured intellectual fighting his own demons, or an arrogant fool. Mephistopheles

can be either a tragic figure in his own right or a scheming demon who has targeted Faustus all along.

Critical history

Academic discussion of the text was first generated when the play was reprinted in 1814. However, it is not satisfactory to judge a play that was written for performance on how it appears on the page, and, without any performances to watch, critics compared Marlowe unfavourably with Shakespeare's later works. Many of the nineteenth-century academics criticised it as 'exceedingly imperfect and disproportioned' (Henry Maitland in 1817), and 'weak and childish' in **style** (Francis Jeffery, also in 1817).

Marlowe's poetry in the soliloquies and serious scenes was praised, however, and William Hazlitt saw that *Doctor Faustus*, 'though an imperfect and unequal performance, is [Marlowe's] greatest work' (1820). He speaks glowingly of Marlowe's achievements, saying: 'There is a lust of power in his writings, a hunger and thirst after unrighteousness, a glow of the imagination, unhallowed by anything but its own energies. His thoughts burn within him like a furnace with bickering flames; or throwing out black smoke and mists, that hide the dawn of genius, or like a poisonous mineral, corrode the heart.'

By the late nineteenth century, the play was discussed on a more complex level. John Addington Symonds saw Faustus as a man who rejected God without denying him. In 1884, he wrote: '*Doctor Faustus* is more nearly allied in dramatic form to the dramatic poems of our own days, which present a psychological study of character to the reader, than any other work of our old theatre.' Marlowe 'left us a picture of the medieval rebel, true in its minutest details to that bygone age, but animated with his own audacious spirit, no longer mythical, but vivified, a living personality'. There was still criticism of the play's construction, however, and in 1893 Sidney Lee condemned *Doctor Faustus* as 'a collection of disconnected scenes rather than a drama'.

Twentieth-century debates

During the first half of the twentieth century, critics continued to express the view that the play invited its readers and audiences to approve of Faustus's aspiration and rebellion. In 1910, George Santayana wrote that 'we like him for his love of life, for his trust in nature, for his enthusiasm for beauty.' He came to the conclusion that 'in a word, Marlowe's Faustus is a martyr to everything that the Renaissance prized — power, curious knowledge, enterprise, wealth and beauty.' In 1927, Una Ellis-Fermor praised 'the logical clearness, the passionate desire for truth, the unswerving courage of his mind', and she questioned the justice of the final scene, concluding that Faustus was a victim, 'a plaything of the gods'.

This interpretation of Faustus as a tragic protagonist brought down by a fatal flaw was disputed by critics such as Leo Kirschbaum who saw the play as the most 'obvious Christian document in all Elizabethan drama'. He wrote: 'For earthly learning, earthly power, earthly satisfaction, Faustus goes down to horrible and everlasting perdition. It does not matter what *you* think of Hell or what Marlowe privately thought of Hell. What does matter is that, in terms of the play, Faustus is a wretched creature who for lower values gives up higher values — that the devil and Hell are omnipresent, potent, and terrifying realities.'

In 1952, Nicholas Brooke wrote an article disagreeing with Kirschbaum, arguing that it is at his moments of repentance that Faustus reveals weakness. 'Marlowe chose deliberately to use the Morality form, and to use it perversely, to invert or at least to satirise its normal intention.' He explains: 'the course of Faustus's resolution is to damn himself; his temptation, his weakness, is in offers of repentance. Faustus's Hell is not at first a place of torture, it is Hell only in that it is absence of Heaven...Heaven is the subjection of self, Hell in this sense is the assertion of self. The foundation of Marlowe's position is that man has certain over-riding desires whose realisation is denied by any form of servitude, and the order of God is, as Milton's Satan observed, an order of servitude.'

Also in 1952, Harry Levin wrote of the play as 'Marlowe's tragedy of the scientific libertine who gained control over nature while losing control of himself'. He picks up the reference in the Prologue to Icarus's 'waxen wings' and links Faustus with other overreachers, saying that 'it is a question of flying too high, of falling from the loftiest height imaginable, of seeking illumination and finding more heat than light'.

Performance criticism

Performance critics hold the view that a play is written to be staged in a theatre and each performance is the result of a unique chemistry between the actors and the audience. Instead of exploring the written text, performance critics explore the play as a living entity, whose interpretation is revealed in all aspects of theatre including casting, costume, set, sound effects and, in the case of *Doctor Faustus*, choice of A-text or B-text. Since the early twentieth century *Doctor Faustus* has become one of the most frequently revived plays by one of Shakespeare's contemporaries and its success depends heavily on the staging. The staging of the play in Chichester in 2004, for instance, was highly innovative and involved members of the local community as devils, angels, sins, kings, queens and so on. Only the initial pact took place in the theatre; the play then turned into a promenade performance through the streets of Chichester, culminating in gorgeous masque-like stagings in the cathedral cloisters and a dramatic denouement in the nave. However, although those members of the audience who knew the play found it most dramatic, others had difficulty following the plot, so perhaps, as an interpretation of the text, the production was not entirely successful.

New Historicism

New Historicism is a school of literary theory that developed in the 1980s, primarily based on the work of the French theorist and critic Roland Barthes and developed by Stephen Greenblatt and others. It aims to understand the literary work through its historical context, and to use the text to shed light on its cultural and historical context. Marlowe's plays are seen as inseparable from the context within which he wrote. Roger Sales, for instance, locates Marlowe's career, both as a dramatist and a spy, within the world of Elizabethan society. He reconstructs the cultural mentality of the Elizabethan spectator through an analysis of the spectacles that were staged by the authorities to both display and maintain their power. He shows how religious and political hostility towards the Elizabethan public theatres was conditioned by a fear that they provided an alternative, or competing, space for spectacle. He argues that Marlowe's major plays indicate that this fear was well-founded since they offered a provocative critique of propaganda in both staged and written forms. They encouraged their audiences to question the theatrical forms, or spectacles, associated with orthodox ideological positions.

Psychoanalytic criticism

Psychoanalytic critics see literature as like dreams. Both are fictions, inventions of the mind that, although based on reality, are by definition not literally true. The theory is that much of what lies in the unconscious mind has been repressed, or censored, by consciousness and emerges only in disguised forms, such as dreams, or in an art form, such as painting or writing. Some critics interpret the author's purpose in writing as being to gratify secretly some forbidden wish that has been repressed into the unconscious mind, so they interpret *Doctor Faustus* as being an expression of Marlowe's own aspirations for knowledge and power and his own ambivalent position concerning orthodox religion.

Psychoanalytic literary criticism can also focus on one or more of the characters; the psychological theory becomes a tool to explain the characters' behaviour and motivations, treating Doctor Faustus and Mephistopheles as real people rather than fictional constructs. Other critics use the theory to explain the appeal of the play for those who read or watch it. *Doctor Faustus* is seen to embody universal human psychological processes and motivations such as religious doubt and the corrupting influence of power, to which the readers respond more or less unconsciously.

Another strand of psychoanalytic criticism is to analyse the role of language and symbolism in the work, exploring, for instance, Faustus's repeated use of the word 'heavenly' in inappropriate contexts. The Good and Evil Angels are often seen as symbolic of Faustus's **psychomachia** (literally 'soul battle') — the inner struggle between Faustus's urge to repent and obtain salvation and his conviction that he is already irrevocably damned. Faustus himself explains this very clearly: 'Hell strives with grace for conquest in my breast.'

Deconstruction

To deconstruct a text is to show that it can have interpretations that are opposites and yet intertwined. *Doctor Faustus* is a play that provokes debate every time it is performed or read; by appearing to support orthodox thinking, Marlowe manages to provoke subversive questioning. Because the play does not have a single 'closed' meaning but obliges each reader to produce her or his own meanings from contradictory suggestions, a deconstructionist refers to it as a 'scriptible' or 'writerly' text rather than a 'lisible' or 'readerly' text, using terms first coined by Barthes in 1970.

Marlowe's language

The English language is constantly evolving and adapting to the world that uses it. Even in your lifetime you will have noticed new words being coined to identify new concepts or inventions, words which change their meaning and some words you used to use that have now fallen out of fashion. It is not surprising then that the language has changed considerably since the Renaissance; perhaps it is more surprising that we can understand so much, finding that the major difficulty for a modern reader is all the classical allusions with which we may be unfamiliar.

As well as the inevitable language change, we need to take into account the fact that Marlowe was writing for the stage. Among other things like costume and make-up, he used language to help him convey the illusion that the principal actor on the stage was actually a brilliant and erudite scholar. As well as using many classical references and quotations from the Bible, Faustus often speaks in blank verse, which gives an elevated **tone** to his discourse. He also speaks fluently in Latin and quotes ancient Greek; most of the audience would not have understood what he was saying, but they would have been deeply impressed by his scholarship and by the sound of his 'mighty verse' ringing round the theatre. Those educated members of the audience would have been flattered into feeling superior, especially when the comic characters made mistakes in their Latin constructions and used the wrong words.

Nowadays there are fixed rules for spelling, punctuation, grammar and **syntax**, but in the sixteenth century there were no dictionaries or grammar books. The only rules Marlowe would have been taught were for the classical languages, and so he had a flexibility that is not available to you in your academic essays. Most of the time, it is possible to work out what the characters are saying without much difficulty, but below you will find some pointers that may help you. There is a glossary starting on page 105 to explain the classical references, because an understanding of them gives extra depth to our appreciation of the play.

Vocabulary

Polysemy

Marlowe frequently chooses words for their multiple meanings, particularly in the comic scenes where plays on words add to the humour. However, he also uses them seriously and we need to be alert to this.

- 'Heavenly' for instance can just mean 'lovely', but it always carries with it the association with the Christian concept of Heaven.
- In line 23 of the Prologue, 'falling' refers back to Icarus dropping into the sea when his wings melt, but, because of the preposition 'to' which follows it, it also looks forward to the metaphorical language of appetite in 'glutted' and 'surfeit'. Compare this with when the Pope encourages his guest to start eating by saying 'fall to' (3.1.76). This is the moment when Faustus 'falls' from a state of grace and 'falls to' the start of his studies on necromancy.
- In 1.3.27, Faustus uses the noun 'virtue'. This word is derived from the Latin for 'manhood, strength', so Faustus is playing on the two meanings of the word; his conjuring has been neither virtuous nor 'heavenly'. The fact that he can joke about what he has done suggests recklessness as well as arrogance.
- In 1.3.15, Faustus uses the verb 'perform' which carries the two meanings of 'accomplish' and 'create with illusions'.
- In 1.3.86, Faustus scornfully tells Mephistopheles to learn 'manly fortitude'. 'Manly' carries the two meanings of masculine as well as human. Marlowe makes Faustus sound recklessly arrogant as he tells one of the angels who fell from heaven to be 'manly'.

Grammar

(1) Second-person singular pronouns and determiners

In Early Modern English — the language of Marlowe's time — there were two forms of second-person singular pronouns and determiners: a *thou*-form (forms with *th-*) and a *you*-form (forms with *y-*). At an earlier time these forms had signalled 'singular' and 'plural' respectively, but in the thirteenth century the plural *you*-form came to be used as a polite form as well — probably in imitation of French, which has familiar *tu* (originally singular) and polite *vous* (originally plural) both possible for singulars.

Examples of *thou*-forms in *Dr Faustus* include:

- Determiners: before a consonant: 'thy studies' (1.1.1), but before a vowel: 'thine incantations' (1.3.5) (NB first-person singular determiner before a vowel is 'mine', e.g. 'mine ears').
- Subject pronoun: 'thou wilt' (1.1.2), 'Wouldst thou' (1.1.24).
- Object pronoun: 'I'll make thee' (1.4.13), 'men…shall appear to thee' (2.1.162).
- Reflexive pronoun: 'Pronounce this thrice devoutly to thyself' (2.1.161).

Modern English has lost this *thou*-form, but in Marlowe's time you could choose which form to use in addressing someone. His way of varying the use of these items can indicate the social class of his characters, as well as characters' attitudes to each other.

In Elizabethan times inferiors would typically use *you* in talking to superiors — as with servants to masters — with *thou* expected in return. However, people also used *thou* to signal special intimacy, such as when addressing God, and it was also normal when lower-class people talked to each other. The upper classes generally used *you* to each other.

Any change from *thou* to *you* or vice versa in a conversation must therefore mean something, conveying a different emotion or mood — perhaps anger, distance or sarcasm.

Examples of normal usage include:

- Superior/inferior: Faustus addresses his servant Wagner with *thou* and receives *you* back, e.g. 'How now Wagner, what's the news with thee?' 'Sir, the Duke of Vanholt doth earnestly entreat your company' (4.1.175–7).
- Faustus addressing God: 'O God, If thou wilt not have mercy on my soul...impose some end to my incessant pain' (5.2.90–93).
- Reciprocal, lower-class: Robin with Rafe, almost always *thou* (e.g. 2.2, 3.2); upper-class: Faustus and Duke of Vanholt consistently *you* (4.2).

  Some significant usages:

- Consistent patterns: Faustus uses *thou* to Mephistopheles, whom he would have as his servant, but the latter consistently uses *thou* back (e.g. 1.3); the Emperor addresses Faustus with *thou*, as if Faustus is of lower status, while Faustus returns *you*, as if he considers the Emperor superior (4.1).
- Change from *thou* to *you* and back again: the servant Wagner addresses Robin, whom he wishes to enlist as his own servant, using *thou*, and Robin obligingly responds with *you* throughout. Only when Wagner directly asks Robin to be his servant does he switch to *you*; when he follows this with a threat he reverts to *thou*: '...bind yourself presently unto me for seven years or I'll turn all the lice about thee into familiars' (1.4.24–26).
- Change from *you* to *thou* to express anger: the Knight uses *you* to Faustus but switches to *thou* when he discovers the trick played on him: 'Do you hear, Master Doctor? You bring Alexander and his paramour before the emperor?' (4.1.53–54), then: 'Thou damnèd wretch and execrable dog...How dar'st thou thus abuse a gentleman?' (4.1.73–75).

Sometimes in Early Modern English the archaic subject pronoun is used with the imperative form of the verb where we normally drop the pronoun altogether, so:

- 'Think thou...' (2.3.71) = Think...!

  also the object pronoun:

- 'haste thee' (1.1.155) = Hurry ...!

(2) Inflected verbs

When Marlowe uses the *thou* form of the second-person singular subject pronoun, he usually uses the appropriate form of the verb, so:

- 'thou wilt' = you will
- 'couldst thou...?' = could you...?
- 'Why wert thou not...?' = Why weren't you...?

However, he uses the subjunctive instead of the inflected form in a conditional construction, e.g.

- 'If thou repent...' (2.3.79)

Marlowe also often uses the appropriate Early Modern English inflected form of the verb with third-person singular subjects, so:

- 'something soundeth...' (2.1.7) = something makes a noise ...
- 'Who buzzeth...?' (2.3.14) = Who buzzes...?

(3) Singular verb forms following plural subjects

This was quite common in the sixteenth century, e.g.

- 'The streets...quarters the town' (3.1.11–12)
- 'her lips sucks' (5.1.93)
- 'see how the heavens smiles' (5.1.116)

(4) Functional variation

The classes into which words fell were sometimes different in Marlowe's time compared to now, so it sometimes appears that Marlowe is using a different part of speech, e.g.

- 'threats the stars' (3.1.18): 'threat' has been superseded by 'threaten' as a verb and is now only used as a noun.
- 'such spirits as can lively resemble Alexander...' (4.1.48): 'lively' is no longer used as an adverb, only as an adjective.
- 'passeth all compare' (5.1.29): the usage of 'compare' as a noun only survives in the phrase 'beyond compare'.
- 'azured arms' (5.1.108): the colour 'azure' is no longer used as a verb. Here it means 'made blue' because Arethusa was turned into water.

(5) Modal auxiliary verbs

Modal auxiliaries are used especially to express gradations of possibility. The first person singular modal 'shall' to express the future tense seems to be falling out of use now. However, the modal still survives in the Ten Commandments to express a command, and also to express emphatic intention in stories such as Cinderella when the fairy godmother declares 'You shall go to the ball'.

Marlowe uses it frequently, e.g.

- 'Mark what I shall say' (4.1.16) indicates the future tense.

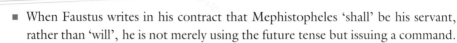

- When Faustus writes in his contract that Mephistopheles 'shall' be his servant, rather than 'will', he is not merely using the future tense but issuing a command.
- Faustus expresses the emphatic intention that 'All things...shall be at my command' (1.1.58–59).

It is always fruitful to explore Marlowe's usage of modal auxiliary verbs and this will gain you good marks for AO2. For instance, in Act 2 scene 3, the Good Angel offers Faustus the comfort that he has not placed himself beyond redemption, but, if he repents, 'God *will* pity thee'. The Evil Angel, however, is more dogmatic: 'God *cannot* pity thee.' At this point Faustus tentatively suggests that 'God *may* pity me' and then more certainly 'God *will* pity me if I repent'. However, the Evil Angel assertively declares: 'Ay, but Faustus never *shall* repent.' Faustus believes this, saying: 'My heart's so hardened I *cannot* repent', but this is not strictly true. He does regret his actions but he never carries this through to full repentance because he is unable to affirm his faith in God's mercy. On line 18, he seems to regret that he '*cannot* repent', but, by line 32, he is expressing determination in 'Faustus *shall* ne'er repent.'

Syntax

(1) Interrogatives
Interrogative forms are made by inverting the subject and the verb rather than by using the auxiliary verb 'do', so:
- 'Think'st thou...?' (1.3.78) for 'Do you think...?'
- 'Who knows not...?' (2.3.50) for 'Who does not know...?'

(2) Negative constructions
Negative constructions are also made without the auxiliary verb 'do', e.g.
- 'That follows not' for 'That does not follow'

Poetry/prose

Marlowe was one of the first Elizabethan dramatists to establish blank verse as the language of plays. Words have a natural **rhythm** that we can see most clearly when we consider a group of words with the same root. The stress pattern of 'rebel' differs according to whether it is used as a noun or a verb. We pronounce 'photograph' with stress on the first and third syllables, but this changes when we add a suffix. In 'photographer' the stress falls on the second syllable, but in 'photographic' we stress the third syllable. Poets harness this natural rhythm and compose lines made up of recurring patterns. The Renaissance playwrights chose the 'iambic' **metre** in which an unstressed syllable is followed by a stressed syllable, reflecting the natural heartbeat: 'baboom baboom' etc. In blank verse, poets put five of these feet in each line, an arrangement called '**iambic pentameter**', and this underlying rhythm gives the speeches a poetic feel so they rarely use **rhyme**.

When a speaker is calm, the heartbeat is regular and speech reflects this; however, Marlowe was the first to demonstrate the potential of blank verse by employing various devices to disrupt the rhythm. In Faustus's final **soliloquy**, for instance, Marlowe inserts short lines, which suggest that his heart misses a beat, and lines longer than the required ten syllables to suggest a heart racing with hope or fear. Sometimes the iambic **foot** is reversed ('Cursed be', 'Adders and serpents', 'Ugly hell') to suggest a thumping heart. Most of the lines are **end-stopped**, and frequent breaks within the lines (mid-line **caesuras**) are created by commands, exclamations or questions to break up the verse, making him sound agitated. However, when Faustus's imagination runs away with him, the lines run on (**enjambement**) to emphasise that his dream of 'Perpetual day' is a hopeless fancy. Thanks to Marlowe's skill as a poet, we not only watch a man in the grip of terror and despair, as audiences had done in earlier plays, we can feel how his agony intensifies as midnight approaches.

In our study of *Doctor Faustus*, we cannot make the sweeping generalisation that Marlowe uses blank verse for educated characters and prose for uneducated ones. The Emperor uses poetry for what appears to be a prepared speech in which he sets out his request, but he uses prose when he is apparently speaking spontaneously. Faustus and Mephistopheles lapse into prose at times when they are having relaxed conversations, so it seems that Marlowe uses verse to heighten the tone of the speech. In the scene with the horse-courser, Marlowe uses prose except for the short soliloquy in the middle of the scene (4.1.126–31). The fact that Marlowe wrote this account of how far Faustus has fallen from his lofty aspirations in poetry has the effect of making the soliloquy even more tense and dramatic in contrast. In Act 5 scene 2 also, Marlowe uses prose for the discussion with the scholars in order to heighten the tension even more when Faustus embarks on his final soliloquy in poetry as the clock strikes 11.

Scene summaries and notes

Prologue

The Chorus, a single actor, enters and prepares the audience for the play to come. It will not be about war, love or heroism, but it will tell the story of an ordinary man who excelled in all his subjects at university. His successes have made him proud and dissatisfied with his studies, so he is about to embark on a study of magic.

- Line 2: Mars was the Roman god of war.
- Line 2: under Hannibal, the Carthaginians defeated the Romans in a battle near Lake Thrasymenus (Trasimene) in 217 BC. No reference to such a play has come down to us.

- Line 6: 'our muse': the Chorus speaks for the company and seems to be crediting the playwright with being their inspiration, like the classical muses.
- Line 12: 'Rhode' = Roda in eastern Germany (now Stadtroda).
- Line 16: at Cambridge, an official 'grace' permits a student to proceed to his degree. Marlowe's name appears in the Grace Book in 1584 and 1587. Note the **pun**.
- Line 20: 'swoll'n with cunning' cf. 1 Corinthians 8:1 'Knowledge puffeth up, but charity edifieth.'
- Line 25: the term 'necromancy', from ancient Greek words for 'the dead' and 'divination' refers to a branch of magic which attempts to raise the spirits of the dead.

Act 1 scene 1

Doctor Faustus is sitting in his study, considering, in a soliloquy, the different branches of learning he has studied. He dismisses all the orthodox subjects, saying that they have nothing to offer him, and then he turns to magic, hoping to become 'a mighty god'. He sends his servant, Wagner, to fetch Valdes and Cornelius to help him learn the art of magic. While he waits, the Good and Evil Angels try to influence him, but there is no evidence that he hears them. He enthuses about everything he will be able to do with his new power, and his visitors enter and offer him fame and fortune. The scene ends with Faustus inviting them to dinner before they teach him what they know, and he vows to conjure that very night.

- Line 1: 'settle thy studies'. From the start of the play, Faustus addresses himself in the second person, conveying his split personality. Ever since Marlowe, writers have used this device to suggest a lack of integrity (see for example *Othello*).
- Line 3: 'commenced' = graduated.
- Line 7: '*Bene disserere est finis logices.*' This quotation comes not from Aristotle but from Petrus Ramus's *Dialecticae*. Ramus, a French humanist, logician and educational reformer, accused Aristotle of inconsistency in his logic.
- Line 12: '*On kai me on*' — Greek for 'to be or not to be'.
- Line 12: Galen was a second-century Greek physician who was the most influential authority on medical science during the Middle Ages and well into the Renaissance.
- Line 19: aphorisms are original thoughts spoken in a short, pithy and memorable form. *Aphorisms* by Hippocrates was the most famous of medical textbooks in the sixteenth century.
- Line 27: Justinian was a Roman emperor of the sixth century who reorganised the whole of Roman law.
- Line 33: 'Church' might be an error for 'law', or Faustus might be being ironic.
- Line 36: 'illiberal' — Faustus sees the law as contrasting with the culturally enriching studies of the liberal arts.

- Line 38: St Jerome's Bible, known as the 'Vulgate', was the Latin translation of the Bible most widely used in Marlowe's day. Marlowe's quotations are not from the Vulgate.
- Lines 39–43: both of Faustus's quotations from the Bible are unfinished. Romans 6:23 states: 'The wages of sin is death, but the gift of God is eternal life through Jesus Christ our Lord.' 1 John 1:8 states: 'If we say that we have no sin, we deceive ourselves and there is no truth in us. If we confess our sins, He is faithful and just to forgive us our sins and to cleanse us from all unrighteousness.' The impression given is that Faustus is weighting the argument to support his decision.
- Line 49: *Che serà, serà* is an Italian proverb.
- Line 58: 'quiet poles' — the poles of the universe are quiet because, unlike the spheres, they are unmoving.
- Line 78: 'Jove' — writers frequently used the names of pagan deities as synonyms for the Christian God, but here the Evil Angel seems to be trying to avoid using God's name.
- Line 80: Marlowe juxtaposes a word from the **semantic field** of appetite, 'glutted', with an abstract concept, 'conceit', in order to emphasise that Faustus's aspirations veer between the intellectual and the sensual. Marlowe neatly shows Faustus confusing the two.
- Line 95: the Prince (actually Duke) of Parma was governor-general of the Spanish Netherlands. In 1588 he was about to invade England, but the defeat of the Armada removed the support of the Spanish navy. He had earlier been responsible for the building of a bridge across the Scheldt in the blockade of Antwerp; this was destroyed by a Dutch fireship in 1589.
- Line 115: 'gravelled' means 'floored or thoroughly defeated in argument'.
- Line 118: Musaeus was a legendary poet and pupil of Orpheus whom Virgil describes in the *Aeneid* surrounded by the spirits of priests and bards in the Greek underworld.
- Line 123: 'Indian Moors' is a reference to Native Americans.
- Line 124: 'the subjects of every element' are the spirits of earth, air, fire and water.
- Line 127: 'Almaine rutters' are German cavalry; the 'staves' are their lances.
- Line 132: Venice was famous for its wealth and the huge merchant ships built there.
- Lines 133–34: 'America the golden fleece/ That yearly stuffs old Philip's treasury'. Gold from America, whose wealth is compared to the legendary golden fleece sought by Jason and the Argonauts, was poured every year into the treasury of King Philip of Spain.
- Line 141: 'tongues' — to converse with spirits it was thought that you needed Greek, Hebrew and Latin.
- Line 145: the most important oracle of the ancient world was at Delphi where people flocked to learn Apollo's wisdom.

- Line 156: 'wise Bacon's and Abanus' works' — Roger Bacon (c. 1210–94) was a Franciscan philosopher who experimented with magic and drew a distinction between legitimate magic and the evil invoking of demons. Pietro d'Abano (1250–1316) was the author of *Heptameron*, a work on conjuring angels. The works of both men would give Faustus formulae for conjuring. As well as these, Faustus would need certain Psalms (especially 22 and 51) and the opening words from St John's Gospel.
- Line 166: 'quiddity' is a philosophical term denoting 'the essence of a thing, that which makes it what it is'.

Act 1 scene 2

Two Scholars ask Wagner where Faustus is. After some joking, he tells them that Faustus is with Cornelius and Valdes. Knowing the latters' reputation for involvement in necromancy, the Scholars fear Faustus may have gone too far to be saved.

- Line 2: '*sic probo*' (Latin): 'thus I prove' is a phrase which signalled the conclusion of a line of argument designed to prove a difficult proposition.
- Line 11: licentiates are graduates permitted to study for a higher degree.
- Lines 19–20: '*corpus naturale…mobile*' (Latin): 'a natural body and capable of movement'.
- Line 26: a 'precisian' is a Puritan; Wagner then mocks the elaborately pious speech of Puritans.
- Line 35: the Rector is the head of the university.

Act 1 scene 3

In the middle of the night, Faustus stands in a magic circle, inscribed with signs and names, which will protect him from evil spirits. He chants in Latin, conjuring up a devil named Mephistopheles who is so horrifyingly ugly that Faustus orders him to change his shape into that of a Franciscan friar. Mephistopheles tells Faustus that he came of his own accord, and that he is a servant of Lucifer, who fell from Heaven because of his pride and insolence. Mephistopheles warns Faustus to abandon his proposed course of action, but Faustus sets out his demands and tells the devil to return at midnight with Lucifer's answer.

- Lines 1–4: it would have been difficult for an Elizabethan theatre to create an appropriate atmosphere because performances took place in the middle of the afternoon and there was no roof. Marlowe, therefore, gives Faustus some awe-inspiring **imagery** and language to open the scene, with an elaborate **personification** of night as a woman, taking a few lines to set an appropriately dark and gloomy scene for conjuring a devil.
- Lines 1–4: Marlowe's description reflects contemporary belief that night was caused by the shadow of the Earth cast by the sun on the heavens, and that this shadow advances from the southern hemisphere.

- Line 2: the constellation of Orion is visible in the winter sky and so was associated with rain.
- Lines 8–13: a magician would draw a circle on the ground around him, inscribing signs and the four Hebrew letters of the Almighty's name, JHWH, and so on, in order to invoke the spirit but also to protect himself.
- Lines 16–22: the Latin invocation can be translated: 'May the gods of Acheron [a river in the Greek underworld] look favourably on me! Let the triple power of Jehovah be strong! Welcome spirit of the fire, of the air, of the water and of the earth! Oh Lucifer, prince of the East, Beelzebub, monarch of burning hell, and Demogorgon favour us so that Mephistopheles may appear and rise up. Why do you delay? By Jehovah, by Gehenna, and by the consecrated water which now I sprinkle, and by the sign of the cross which now I make and by our vows, may Mephistopheles himself now rise at our command.'
- Lines 19–22: after invoking the triple power of Jehovah (God, the father, God, the son, and the Holy Ghost), Faustus invokes the triple power of Satan. According to Isaiah 14:12–15, Lucifer (Latin for 'light-bearer') was 'son of the morning', so prince of the East; Isaiah gives an account of his fall. The name 'Beelzebub' possibly comes from the Hebrew for 'lord of things that fly' and was popularly named 'Lord of the Flies'. Beelzebub was one of the fallen angels and Lucifer's chief lieutenant. 'Demogorgon' is the name of a pagan demon associated with the underworld and envisaged as a powerful primordial being; the name possibly derives from the ancient Greek for 'grim demon'.
- Line 19: 'Mephistopheles', possibly from the ancient Greek for 'no friend to light', was a name coined by the author of the *Faustbuch*.
- Line 20: 'Gehenna' is the Jewish equivalent of Hell. In ancient times, children were sacrificed to the pagan god Moloch in the valley of Hinnom, near Jerusalem. Fires were kept burning there, and Hinnom became the rubbish dump for the city, metaphorically identified with the underworld.
- The English translation of the *Faustbuch* describes a creature of fire coming in answer to Faustus's conjuring. The B-text specifies that Mephistopheles comes in the shape of a dragon.
- Line 26: Marlowe takes the opportunity to make an anti-Catholic joke that Franciscan friars are immoral, but this has a more serious function in showing how Faustus cannot confront the consequences of his actions directly, needing them to be presented in a pleasing manner.
- Line 34: '*Quin redis, Mephistopheles, fratris imagine!*' means 'Why do you not return, Mephistopheles, in the likeness of a friar?'
- Line 46: '*per accidens*' means 'as it happens'; Mephistopheles is making it clear that he did not come because Faustus summoned him but because Faustus was putting his soul in danger.
- Line 60: Elysium is where the ancient Greeks believed they would live after death.

- Line 61: Faustus may be thinking of 'the old philosophers' whom he would meet in Elysium if it existed, or he may be identifying himself with those who share his disbelief in the concept of an eternity of punishment.
- Line 68: pride was thought to be the most serious of the Seven Deadly Sins because it meant setting yourself up against God. Insolence was a much more powerful concept in Marlowe's day, implying an overbearing arrogance.
- Lines 71–73: Marlowe enhances the poignancy of Mephistopheles' regret by using an epistrophe, in which a series of lines end with the same two words.
- Line 77: Mephistopheles's description of Hell as a state of mind is a translation of St John Chrysostom's words '*si decem mille Gehennas quis dixerit, nihil tale est quale ab illa beata visione excidere*'. Chrysostom, Archbishop of Constantinople in the fourth century, was a famously eloquent preacher.
- Line 92: Why 24 years? Twenty-four (12 x 2) and 12 are symbolic and spiritual numbers; 12 stands for governmental perfection, there are 12 apostles and 12 tribes of Israel, and so 24 stands for double perfection; it is a travesty of holiness to do a deal with the devil for 24 years. The number might have been suggested by the hours in a day, so it could be both a metaphorical reminder that it is a short space of time as well as suggesting a continuous cycle. However, in the plague-ridden sixteenth century, Faustus could be asking for a guarantee that he will live to a ripe old age!
- Line 106: Faustus's plans to 'make a bridge through the moving air' may have been suggested by the example of the Persian emperor Xerxes, who constructed a bridge of boats across the Hellespont so that his army could cross it. Marlowe is making an ironic parallel with Satan, who builds a bridge from Hell to Earth.

Act 1 scene 4

Faustus's servant, Wagner, persuades Robin, a country bumpkin, to become his servant by conjuring up devils and offering to teach the 'Clown' to turn himself into any kind of animal.

- Line 5: Robin plays on the words 'goings out', meaning both expenses and holes in his clothes.
- Lines 13–14: '*Qui mihi discipulus*' is Latin for 'You who are my disciple'. These are the first words of a poem by William Lily, a schoolmaster, often used in schools.
- Line 16: 'beaten silk and stavesacre' — Wagner offers to dress his servant handsomely in silk which has had gold or silver hammered into it for decoration, but he will also need a preparation made from delphinium seeds which was used to kill fleas. The choice of the word 'beaten' also suggests that this is how he will treat his new servant.
- Line 17: Robin turns this insult back on Wagner by pretending that he thought

Wagner said 'knavesacre', which was the six feet of land required to bury someone, however poor or criminal.

- Line 26: 'familiars' are agents of the devil in the form of animals.
- Lines 30–35: To bind Robin to him as a servant, Wagner offers him guilders, which are Dutch coins. Wagner reveals his ignorance by calling them French crowns, but Robin knows that they are easily counterfeited and probably worthless. In 1587, the government urged anyone offered a counterfeit coin to pierce a hole in it.
- Line 32: Robin mispronounces the word 'guilders' as 'gridirons' — implements used for spit-roasting meat; they were also used by torturers and would therefore have been used in Hell. Robin may also be referring to the mutilation of counterfeit coins.
- Line 44: 'Balioll and Belcher' — Wagner seems to be mispronouncing the names of devils, possibly Belial and Beelzebub. Marlowe, a Cambridge University graduate, may be making a joke directed at Balliol College, Oxford.
- In the stage direction, 'crying' means shouting and yelling rather than weeping.
- Lines 53–4: Robin indulges in sexual innuendo, making crude remarks concealed as comments on the 'horns' (also worn by cuckolds) and cloven feet of devils ('cleft' can refer both to the slit in the hoof and to the vulva). 'Plackets', slits in skirt fronts, is another bawdy pun as it was also a slang term for the vagina.
- Lines 70–71: '*quasi vestigiis nostris insistere*' — Wagner's Latin is not accurate, but he means to say 'as it were tread in my footsteps'.
- Line 72: 'Dutch fustian' — as in the phrase 'double Dutch', Robin refers to Wagner's attempt at Latin as gibberish. 'Fustian' is both coarse cloth and pretentious speech.

Act 2 scene 1

After much wavering, Faustus writes a contract in his own blood giving both body and soul to Lucifer in exchange for Mephistopheles as 'his servant, and at his command'. In exchange, he learns about the existence of Hell and is given 'a devil dressed like a woman with fireworks' when he asks for a wife. Mephistopheles gives him books about magic, astronomy and botany, but he seems troubled.

- Line 10: 'The god thou servest is thine own appetite'. Faustus realises that his course of action will not enable him to climb higher in the Great Chain of Being, which is what he wanted to do when he urged himself to 'try thy brains to gain a deity'. Instead, he is sinking lower and becoming more like an animal that seeks only to satisfy its physical cravings.
- Line 23: 'seigniory of Emden' — governorship of Emden, a prosperous German port. However, as the play progresses, it emerges that Faustus does not want political power. After signing the contract, he does nothing to gain it, but the possibility is important to him.

- Line 29: '*Veni, veni, Mephistophile!*' — Latin for 'Come, come, Mephistopheles!'
- Line 42: '*Solamen miseris socios habuisse doloris.*' — Latin for 'it is solace to the wretched to have had companions in sorrow'.
- Line 74: '*Consummatum est*'— Latin for 'it is completed'. Faustus blasphemously uses the last words of Christ on the cross.
- Line 77: '*Homo, fuge!*' — Latin for 'Man, fly!' This command seems ambiguous; it could mean either 'Fly from what you are doing' or 'Fly from the wrath of God'. However, the words are taken from 1 Timothy 6:11: 'But thou, O man of God, flee these things; and follow after righteousness, godliness, faith, love, patience, meekness.'
- Line 97: 'a spirit in form and substance' — to the Elizabethans, a spirit was usually evil. Having given both body and soul to Lucifer, to the orthodox Faustus would be instantly damned. Although God was still prepared to forgive, the fallen angels and those who joined them lacked the capacity to repent and affirm their faith in God's mercy.

Act 2 scene 2

Although this scene follows the next scene in the A-text, modern editors often place it here because it reworks the themes of the previous scene and creates a time lapse before Faustus's realisation that he has not gained what he wanted from the contract. Robin has stolen one of Faustus's books of magic, and he is boasting to Rafe about what he will be able to achieve with it.

- Line 2 etc.: 'circles', 'things', 'chafing', 'bear with me', 'turn', 'wind' — note the **double entendre**.
- Line 15: the 'forehead' is where a cuckold's horns are said to grow when his wife has been unfaithful to him.
- Line 24: 'nothing' also carries a sexual meaning as a woman has 'no thing'.

Act 2 scene 3

Wondering at the stars, Faustus curses Mephistopheles for having deprived him of the joys of Heaven. For the third time he is visited by the Good and Evil Angels. He thinks of repentance but decides that he cannot repent and consoles himself with debating astronomy with Mephistopheles. Eventually he comes to the question of who made the world and this makes him doubt once again. Another visit by the Angels prompts him to begin to repent, but Lucifer arrives and distracts him with a show of the Seven Deadly Sins. Lucifer gives Faustus another book and he is content.

- Line 1: 'repent' — to an Elizabethan Christian, repentance means 1) acknowledgement of sin, 2) confession before God, 3) affirmation of faith in God's mercy, 4) amendment of sinful ways.
- Lines 21–23: 'swords and knives,/ Poison, guns, halters, and envenomed steel/

Are laid before me to dispatch myself'. This long list allows the actor to build up to a **climax**, revealing Faustus's suicidal paranoia, because we only witness Mephistopheles offering Faustus one dagger to kill himself.

- Line 28: 'he that built the walls of Thebes' — Amphion, son of Zeus, was a brilliant musician, playing so beautifully on his lyre that, when he and his brother built a wall round Thebes, the stones were so affected by his music that they fitted themselves into place of their own accord.
- Line 35: 'heavens above the moon' — heavens here refers to the spheres in which it was believed that the planets and stars were set. It was believed that the 'centric' Earth was at the centre of the universe, beyond the Earth was the sphere of the Moon and further out still the spheres of the other planets (or 'erring stars'). The eighth sphere was the 'firmament', or sphere of fixed stars, and the ninth was the 'empyreal heaven', which was where God lived. Mephistopheles explains that the spheres enclose each other and all rotate upon a single 'axletree'.
- Line 38: 'As are the elements' — the elements were also thought to enclose each other. Earth is surrounded by water, water by air and air by fire.
- Line 44: '*situ et tempore*' — Latin for 'in direction and time'. Faustus asks whether the planets move in the same direction and at the same speed. Mephistopheles explains that the planets have 'double motion' – they revolve from the west to the east every 24 hours on the Earth's axis, and then they rotate from east to west at different speeds on the axis of the universe.
- Lines 55–56: 'hath every sphere a dominion or *intelligentia*?' There was a theory that each planet was guided by an angelic spirit or *intelligence*.
- Line 62: 'conjunctions' are when two heavenly bodies appear to have the same longitude, or to be joined together.
- Line 62: 'oppositions' are when their longitude appears to differ by 180°.
- Line 62: the 'aspect' is the relative position of heavenly bodies, measured by angular distance.
- Line 64: '*Per inaequalem motum respectu totius*'— Latin for 'through unequal motion in respect of the whole'. Mephistopheles tells Faustus what he already knows — that there are more irregularities such as eclipses in some years than others, because the heavenly bodies move at different speeds.
- Line 84: 'int'rest' — a legal claim.
- Lines 108–09: 'Ovid's flea' — this is a reference to a poem in Latin, *Elegia de Pulice*, wrongly attributed to Ovid, in which the envious poet complains to the flea, 'you go wherever you want. Nothing is hidden from you, you savage'.
- Line 113: 'cloth of arras' — tapestry woven in Arras, Flanders (now in northern France) and used for wall-hangings.
- Line 116: 'old leathern bag' — a miser's purse.
- Line 140: 'Martlemas-beef' refers to cattle slaughtered around St Martin's Day (11 November), which was salted to preserve it for the winter.

- Line 142: 'March-beer' was a strong beer that was brewed in March and left to mature for a couple of years.
- Line 152: 'raw mutton' was slang for lust.
- Line 153: 'stockfish', a long strip of dried cod, was a common insult inferring impotence.

Act 3 Chorus

The actor playing Wagner invites members of the audience to use their imaginations as he describes what Faustus has been doing since he signed the contract. A chariot drawn by dragons has taken him to the top of Mount Olympus to learn the secrets of astronomy, and now he is in Rome to test his knowledge of the physical world.

- Line 3: Jove was the name Romans gave to their supreme deity. Here it is being used as a synonym for the Christian God.
- Line 4: 'Did mount himself to scale Olympus' top'. This does not refer to the actual mountain in Greece but to the home of the Greek gods. It suggests that Faustus has learned knowledge about astronomy which only God has.
- Lines 5–6: 'a chariot burning bright/ Drawn by the strength of yoky dragons' necks'. Faustus has had such an exciting time that even mythical creatures are subservient to him. Dragons are yoked together like oxen so that the chariot bearing him can fly to real and, possibly, mythical places.
- Line 10: 'holy Peter's feast' — Peter was one of Christ's apostles and the first Bishop of Rome. St Peter's Day is 29 June.

Act 3 scene 1

Faustus describes his travels appreciatively, and Mephistopheles tells him about Rome. Faustus is keen to see the sights, but his companion suggests that they have some fun at the Pope's expense. At the banquet, Faustus is invisible and plays tricks on the Pope and his guest. Friars chant a ritual curse and Faustus and Mephistopheles beat them and fling fireworks.

- Faustus has been on a tour of Europe, from Trier (Trèves) in western Germany, to Paris in France, then back to Germany to where the River Main joins the River Rhine. Next he went to Naples, in the region of Campania in southern Italy, to Padua and Venice in northern Italy and back south to Rome.
- Line 13: 'learnèd Maro' — the Roman poet Publius Virgilius Maro (Virgil) was buried in Naples at the end of a promontory between Naples and Pozzuoli. Virgil was thought to have been a magician, and the mile-long tunnel that runs through this rocky promontory was attributed to his magic art.
- Line 17: 'a sumptuous temple' — this is probably St Mark's in Venice.
- Line 37: 'Ponte Angelo' — the Ponte Sant'Angelo was built across the River Tiber in AD 135 by Hadrian. The Castello di Sant'Angelo is not actually built on the bridge but directly facing it.

- Line 42: 'high pyramides' — there are eight ancient Egyptian obelisks in Rome. The gilt ball at the top of the obelisk in St Peter's Square was believed to contain the ashes of Julius Caesar, but this has since been disproved.
- Lines 44–46: Faustus swears by 'the kingdoms of infernal rule,/ Of Styx, Acheron, and the fiery lake/ Of ever-burning Phlegethon'. These are the rivers of Hades, the Greek underworld, so this is an appropriate oath for someone who has forsworn God and his Heaven. Plato saw the Phlegethon as the source of the streams of lava that spout up at various places on earth.
- Line 53: '*summum bonum*'— Latin for 'the greatest good'; this is a theological term referring to the goodness of God.
- Line 58: Ironically, Mephistopheles is dressed as a friar (1.3.25) as they play tricks on the friars.
- Line 60: Marlowe has chosen to show the Pope and his guest at a banquet, continuing the imagery of over-eating that was introduced in the Prologue and firmly established when Gluttony paraded in front of Faustus.
- Line 81: '*Faustus hits him a box of the ear*' — this humiliation of the Roman Catholic Pope is a way of showing the ungodliness of Faustus without upsetting the authorities in Protestant England. It would also have been a way of adding to the fear engendered by this play, because even Protestants would be nervous to see a representative of God on earth being mocked.
- Lines 82–83: 'We shall be cursed with bell, book and candle' — at the close of the Office of Excommunication that ceremonially excludes someone from the Church, a bell is tolled, a Bible is closed and a candle is extinguished. Queen Elizabeth had been excommunicated by the Pope in 1570. They are also necessary objects for an exorcism.
- Line 90: '*Maledicat Dominus*' — Latin for 'May the Lord curse him'. Faustus's tricks are petty, but they are a way of showing up the pettiness of the papal court which degrades the rituals of the Church to revenge in excommunicating the one who stole the Pope's meat and drink. More importantly, the Pope is powerless to defend himself against Faustus because he is already damned.
- Line 99: '*Et omnes sancti*' — Latin for 'and all the saints'.

Act 3 scene 2

Robin and Rafe are challenged by the vintner for their theft of a goblet. They deny it and then Robin tries conjuring. His garbled incantation succeeds in raising Mephistopheles who punishes them.
- Line 2: '*Ecce signum*' — Latin for 'behold the sign'.
- Lines 10–11: 'a etc.' — an invitation for the comedian to extemporise, or to ad-lib.
- Line 25: '*Sanctobulorum Periphrasticon!*' — 'thesaurus of the saints' — a mixture of Latin and Greek.

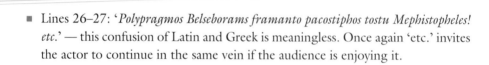

- Lines 26–27: '*Polypragmos Belseborams framanto pacostiphos tostu Mephistopheles! etc.*' — this confusion of Latin and Greek is meaningless. Once again 'etc.' invites the actor to continue in the same vein if the audience is enjoying it.

Act 4 Chorus

It is through the Chorus that the audience learns what Faustus has gained by his contract. On his travels, Faustus has seen 'the rarest things', but now he has returned home to Wittenberg, where he has been warmly greeted. Faustus's learning is spectacularly improved, and he is now famous throughout the world. The Chorus introduces the next scene in which Faustus has been invited to the court of Charles V, the Holy Roman Emperor, at Innsbruck.

Act 4 scene 1

Faustus and Mephistopheles provide a magic show for the Emperor, conjuring up spirits who are identical to Alexander the Great and his 'paramour'. Faustus is annoyed by a knight who mocks him, and he causes horns to grow on the man's head. Faustus is aware that his time is running out and sets off to walk home. A horse-dealer pesters him and Faustus plays tricks on him.

- Line 9: 'prejudiced or endamaged' — the Emperor offers Faustus legal immunity for practising necromancy.
- Line 35: 'paramour' — this word has since narrowed in meaning. In Marlowe's day it meant 'beloved', from the French 'by love', so it probably refers to Alexander's first wife, Roxana.
- Line 60: 'I'll meet with you' means 'I'll get even with you'.
- Stage direction: '*a pair of horns*' — according to the **conventions** of stage comedy, this was a sign that a man had been 'cuckolded' because his wife had been unfaithful. The horns suggest that the husband has become a tamed beast or farmyard animal and, like them, he is ignorant because everyone can see his horns except himself.
- Line 71: 'bachelor' — this joke relies on the two meanings: 1) an unmarried man, 2) a trainee knight.
- Line 94: 'thread of vital life' — in Greek mythology, the Fates were said to spin a thread for each person's life and cut it at the end of the allotted span.
- Line 100: 'Horse-courser' — horse dealers have long had a reputation for dishonesty.
- Line 105: 'dollar' was the English name for the 'thaler', a German coin.
- Line 114: running water is said to dissolve spells.
- Line 115: 'drink of all waters' — a proverbial expression meaning 'go anywhere, do anything'.
- Lines 120–21: 'hey, ding, ding' — a slang term for a penis (now more usually

'ding-a-ling'). The horse dealer wishes the horse had not been gelded so that he could use it as a stud (note the sexual innuendo of 'slick buttock' and 'eel').

- Line 130: 'Christ did call the thief upon the cross' — according to St Luke's Gospel (23:43), Jesus comforted one of the crucified thieves saying: 'Verily I say unto thee, today shalt thou be with me in paradise.'
- Lines 132–33: 'Doctor Lopus' — Dr Rodrigo Lopez, a Portuguese Jew, was at this time Queen Elizabeth's personal physician. In 1594, he was hanged, drawn and quartered at Tyburn for allegedly trying to poison her, so this joke seems to be a later addition.
- Line 133: 'purgation' — a medical term for 'giving an emetic to empty the bowels'.
- Line 143: 'hey-pass' — a conjuror's expression similar to 'hey presto'.
- Line 149–50: 'glass windows' — Faustus is wearing glasses.

Act 4 scene 2

Marlowe shows us one of the wonders Faustus performed for the Duke and Duchess of Vanholt, providing grapes in winter.

- Line 1: 'hath much' — we join the characters in the middle of Faustus's visit, after he has already entertained his hosts with magic.
- Line 5: 'great-bellied' — pregnant. There was no disrespect in this description.
- Line 20: 'two circles' — Faustus explains about the two hemispheres. He may be confused, speaking of East and West rather than North and South; however in the B-text there is no confusion as there is an extra line: '…as in India, Saba, and such countries that lie far east, where they have fruit twice a year. From whence, by…'

Act 5 scene 1

Wagner is confused by Faustus's behaviour. Faustus has given Wagner all his things as if he is about to die, but he is carousing with the students. Faustus conjures a vision of Helen of Troy for some Scholars. An old man exhorts him to repent, but Mephistopheles invites Faustus to kill himself, threatens to tear his flesh, makes him cut his arm and sign the contract again, and finally brings back Helen to distract Faustus from thoughts of repentance. The old man is tortured by devils but dies happy, interpreting the torture as God's test of his faith.

- Line 4: 'carouse and swill' — these verbs suggest a rowdy and drunken party.
- Line 68: 'Revolt' — turn again, back to allegiance to Lucifer.
- Line 91: 'topless towers of Ilium' — Marlowe suggests that the towers of Troy (Ilium) are so high that their tops cannot be seen. This is a symbol for limitless aspiration.
- Line 96: 'dross' — the scum left behind when precious metals are heated to purify them.

Act 5 scene 2

Faustus explains his predicament to the Scholars. He tries to pray, but devils are already controlling his body, and he is unable to weep, pray or raise his hands to Heaven. He sends the Scholars away for their safety, asking them to pray for him. The clock strikes eleven. Faustus spends his final hour looking for ways to escape an eternity in Hell. At midnight, there is thunder and lightning and devils take him away.

- Line 66: '*O lente, lente currite noctis equi!*' — 'Go slowly, slowly you horses of the night!' A quotation from Ovid's *Amores* in which the poet, lying in his mistress's arms, wishes the night would never end.
- Line 99: 'Pythagoras' *metempsychosis*' — a Greek philosophical term referring to the theory that the human soul transmigrates after death into some other form of life, in a constant process of reincarnation and purification.
- Line 103: 'elements' — earth, air, fire and water.
- Line 109: 'quick' — alive. This meaning now survives in the 'quick' of the nail.

Epilogue

The Chorus returns to lament the tragic fall of a brilliant man and to warn the audience to learn from Faustus's example.

- Line 2: 'Apollo's laurel bough' — in ancient Greece, a laurel was given to those who excelled in their field, so we are reminded of Faustus's first soliloquy in which he gives details of his success in the field of medicine.
- Line 7: 'forward wits' — presumptuous academics.
- '*Terminat hora diem; terminat author opus*' — Latin for 'the hour ends the day; the author ends his work'. This motto may have been added by the printer.

Character notes

Doctor Faustus

Doctor Faustus is an ordinary man, 'base of stock', who spends 30 years (5.2.18) at Wittenberg University. When the play opens, he has been awarded the title of Doctor for his studies in Divinity, but he has also been successful in the fields of Logic, Medicine and the Law. He is disillusioned with academic life, dissatisfied with his achievements and searching for something more. He turns to magic and necromancy to satisfy his ambitions, and writes a contract in his own blood that trades his soul for 24 years with Mephistopheles to wait on him. He ignores Mephistopheles's warning that he is servant to Lucifer and can only perform what Lucifer allows. Faustus becomes famous throughout the known world for his learning, and he delights people with his magic, but he is unable to affirm his faith in God's mercy, believing himself to be irrevocably damned, and so, at the end, devils take him to Hell.

Mephistopheles

Mephistopheles fell from heaven with Lucifer. When he hears Faustus 'rack the name of God', he comes in the hope of getting Faustus's soul to enlarge Lucifer's kingdom. Mephistopheles is unhappy at being deprived of the joys of Heaven, and at first he tries to dissuade Faustus from his chosen course. However, once he has been back to Lucifer to arrange the contract, he does everything necessary to get Faustus's soul. When Faustus begins to repent, Mephistopheles brings Lucifer to distract him. When the Old Man tries to persuade Faustus to repent, Mephistopheles offers Faustus a dagger. He answers all Faustus's questions and fulfils all his commands, as long as they do not go against Lucifer's kingdom. In the penultimate scene, he brings a devil in the likeness of Helen of Troy to tempt Faustus into demoniality, the bodily intercourse with spirits, after which there can be no forgiveness.

The Chorus

The Chorus is an actor who introduces and ends the play by addressing the audience directly. He explains what the audience is about to watch, fills in the gaps in the story and tells the audience how they should react. In the Prologue and Epilogue, he disapproves of Faustus, which suggests that these speeches would be spoken by a different actor than the other Chorus speeches spoken at the beginnings of Act 3 (Wagner) and Act 4.

Wagner

Wagner has two functions. In 1.2, he is part of the comic tradition of the cheeky lower-class servant who ridicules his social superiors and exposes them to the audience's mockery. However, he is always loyal to Faustus and never makes jokes at his expense. In 1.4, he is, in his turn, the butt of jokes made by Robin, who is of a lower social status than himself and exposes Wagner's pretensions. In these scenes, Marlowe uses him to expose Faustus's pretensions, reminding the audience that he will be merely the servant of Lucifer. Through him, Marlowe reveals how easy it is to conjure devils. You do not need great learning nor a close study of demonology, as Faustus thinks. Even simple men are in danger, serving to demonstrate how Faustus is corrupting the morals of others.

In the Act 3 Chorus and 5.1, Wagner is a commentator on the action, revealing admiration for his master, an intellectual curiosity of his own, and puzzlement at Faustus's strange behaviour. He has some of the functions of the Chorus in giving a sense of the passing of time, filling in gaps in the story and revealing what Faustus actually gains from his contract with Lucifer.

The Good and Evil Angels

The Good and Evil Angels are the counterparts of the virtues and vices personified in the morality plays of the Middle Ages. They also represent Faustus's conscience and his appetite. The Good Angel is the dramatic representation of God's Truth and repeatedly gives voice to the possibility of repentance and forgiveness. It stresses the supremacy of the individual's freedom of choice. The Evil Angel tempts Faustus with knowledge and power, reputation and wealth, and threatens him with physical torture. It dismisses contrition, prayer and repentance as 'illusions' and 'fruits of lunacy' and reinforces Faustus's belief that God cannot pity him, and that he is incapable of true repentance.

There are two possible interpretations of the Good and Evil Angels. They can be presented as separate characters in their own right, following in the morality play tradition of having allegorical figures whom the protagonist meets on his journey through life. Alternatively, they can be presented as mouthpieces for Faustus's own thoughts, performing the same function as a soliloquy, with the two sides of Faustus's mind vying for control.

The speeches of the Angels create a pause in the action during which the audience is invited to reflect on Faustus's moral situation. They always appear together, have no names and could be indistinguishable on stage. Alternatively, they could be dressed to represent visually the influence they seek to exert, or they could even be presented as comic caricatures. Either way, they serve to distance the audience from Faustus, as their appearances on stage remind us of an older dramatic tradition based on the belief that this life is a preparation for an afterlife in Heaven or Hell, and that the powers of each do battle for our souls.

Valdes and Cornelius

Valdes and Cornelius are well known to be magicians. They lend Faustus their books and teach him how to conjure spirits. Together with Faustus, Cornelius and Valdes make up the traditional unholy trinity, like the three drunken rioters in Chaucer's *The Pardoner's Tale*. In each case, the unholy trinity has been given gifts, either education or gold, and yet they all desire to have more than they are permitted. They function like the vice crew in the morality plays, tempting Faustus and flattering him by saying that they need his intelligence to achieve the greatest powers. However, they conjure spirits not devils. Faustus has already decided to pursue magic and does not need to be tempted, so it seems that Marlowe is using them to help Faustus to convince the audience that the idea of magical powers is ravishing. There is a limit to the actual conjuring the actors can do on stage, so, like Faustus, they have speeches filled with excitement and anticipation, filled with glorious images.

Valdes and Cornelius do not appear in Marlowe's source text; Marlowe seems to have invented them to help Faustus to convey the excitement of magic.

Dramatically, it is more interesting to have two other characters sharing his pleasurable anticipation. Valdes yearns for fame, power and wealth; Cornelius longs for the knowledge that will lead to a worldwide reputation and power over spirits. Like Faustus, they do not want any specific thing. Valdes tempts Faustus with fame, fortune and beautiful women, whereas Cornelius seems to understand him better, laying emphasis on knowledge and the possibility of Faustus being able to 'try his cunning by himself'. They only appear once, and this contributes to the sense of Faustus's isolation once he has signed the contract. Their presence shows that Faustus is not the only one who has succumbed to temptation. They also reveal Faustus to be exceptionally able, since they seem to think that they are unable to achieve what they want without Faustus, whereas Faustus works alone.

The Scholars

The Scholars are 'licentiate'; this means that they have already gained their first degree and are permitted to study for a higher degree. In 1.2, they are comic characters whom Wagner has no trouble holding up to ridicule. They serve to show how much admired Faustus is for his great learning as well as his magic. They are presumably the 'friends and nearest companions' who welcome Faustus's return to Wittenberg, according to Chorus 4. These nameless students are also the people with whom Faustus spends his final night on Earth, emphasising his loneliness. They function as the prompt for the conjuring of Helen of Troy.

They are strongly religious and, in the final scene, act like the Good Angel in reminding Faustus that God's mercies are infinite. Once they know what Faustus has done, they realise that he is beyond redemption, but one, whose faith is particularly strong, offers to stay with him, giving him companionship until the end. Significantly, Faustus does not reject this offer, but another, more cautious Scholar intervenes and then Faustus reinforces his warning. Because of the Scholars, Faustus is not entirely devoid of human company as his end approaches.

Robin

Robin has plenty of native **wit** and provides the bawdy humour in his scene with Wagner (1.4), who is showing off in front of the country bumpkin. Robin mocks devils but learns by experience to fear them, and even he is able to conjure Mephistopheles. Robin has had less education than Wagner; he cannot read but he has picked up some dog-Latin phrases. He seems to have newly arrived in Wittenberg from the country and uses old-fashioned Roman Catholic oaths; his clothes are ragged and he looks hungry.

Wagner employs him as a servant, and the next time we see Robin he has stolen one of Faustus's conjuring books. This time it is his turn to show off in front of Rafe (2.2), and the scene serves to reveal that Faustus's achievements are not reserved

for exceptionally talented men. In 3.2, Marlowe has him steal a goblet, suggesting that Faustus's mockery of the Pope and his guest is no more than theft. This also demonstrates that the corruption initiated by Faustus is spreading further down the social scale. Robin is a cheerful, pragmatic character who finds the advantage of being transformed into an ape.

Robin is punished by Mephistopheles for the presumption of summoning him. If the theft of the cup presents a parallel to Faustus's theft of the Pope's meat and drink, then Marlowe's treatment of Robin raises the anticipation of what punishment Faustus will suffer for his presumption.

Rafe

Rafe is a common man who is led astray by Robin, who involves him in his mischievous thieving from and lying to the vintner. Unlike Robin, he makes no bawdy jokes and puns, but he is also lecherous. Robin and Rafe represent ordinary people, but they also hold a distorting mirror up to Faustus's lowly birth, his ambition, his persuadability and his sexual appetite.

Lucifer

Lucifer is 'arch-regent and commander of all spirits'. Reading his speeches he sounds like an unimpressive entertainer, but the actor would have looked truly terrifying and no doubt used a voice to match his appearance.

The Pope and the Cardinal of Lorraine

The Pope and the Cardinal of Lorraine are comic figures who represent the Roman Catholic Church. Through these characters, Marlowe satirises those men of the Church who indulge their appetites to excess, like Chaucer's Monk who 'A fat swan loved…best of any roost'. The gluttonous Pope keeps trying to eat and drink, and he urges his guest to do so in spite of the food and drink being snatched out of their hands. However, this is not just gluttony but a travesty of the communion service. Finally, the Friars chant the Office of Excommunication in petty revenge for the theft of the Pope's food and the assault on his dignity. As well as being a satire on the self-indulgence of churchmen, this scene has a more serious point in exposing how powerless the Church is against those who are already damned.

Marlowe is pleasing the Protestant audience by exposing the Roman Catholic Church to ridicule, but he is also creating more dramatic tension by making a fool out of the one character in the play who represents the Christian religion. Mephistopheles and Faustus, the representatives of the Devil, run rings round all the religious characters; they have no difficulty in triumphing over the powers of Christian religion. The Friars are given an impressive-sounding chant with ridiculously trivial words to make them figures of fun.

The Vintner

The Vintner is dignified and polite, but he stands up for himself.

The Emperor

The Emperor is Charles V, Holy Roman Emperor, the father of Philip II of Spain, whose Armada was defeated by Elizabeth's forces in 1588, probably just before Marlowe wrote *Doctor Faustus*. Charles is proud of his ancestors, especially Alexander the Great, but he is polite and gracious to Faustus, offers him political immunity for what he is about to do, and rewards him generously. He has a sense of humour and enjoys the joke against the Knight, although he begs Faustus to release the Knight from the spell. The scene in which Faustus humbly entertains the Emperor reminds the audience of how different Faustus's life has been from the one he planned in 1.1. For all his skill, Faustus is not the Emperor's equal; in fact, he is pleased to be invited to perform tricks, and he speaks humbly and subserviently.

The Knight

The Knight is made a laughing stock but reveals how little Faustus can actually achieve. The presence of the Knight in 4.1 emphasises not the great respect that Faustus commands, but the accompanying cynicism. The Knight expresses his cynicism in a way that might be considered either brave or foolhardy, but it reinforces the audience's feeling that Faustus is not a mighty god but a lowly conjuror. When the Knight feels the horns, he is angry and abusive rather than apologetic. Marlowe draws a comparison between the Knight and Actaeon, who, like Faustus, lusted after something forbidden and, on attaining it, was destroyed by it.

The Horse-courser

The Horse-courser is a stereotypically dishonest dealer who hopes to cheat Faustus but gets the worst of the bargain. He serves to illustrate how low Faustus has fallen. This scene indicates Faustus's descent to the level of the lower classes, playing tricks for trifling sums of money, not unlike the thefts attempted by Robin and Rafe. Not only has Faustus not achieved the political power he anticipated, but he is revealed to be no more than a common trickster. Just as the Horse-courser has bought what he thinks is a horse but turns out to be a bale of hay, so Faustus erroneously thinks he has bought unlimited power and knowledge with his soul.

Duke and Duchess of Vanholt

Duke and Duchess of Vanholt are polite to Faustus and appreciative of his efforts, but this emphasises that he serves others rather than wielding power himself. They are less powerful and lower in social status than the Emperor, and yet Faustus is still humble towards them. He is grateful for an invitation from a duke, and all the aspirations he expressed in the first scene are now forgotten.

The Old Man

The Old Man is an enigmatic figure, belonging to a literary tradition of wise, old, nameless characters who accept God's will unquestioningly and have some kind of symbolic role. In *The Pardoner's Tale*, Chaucer includes an old man who tells three drunken young revellers where they can find Death and directs them to a pile of gold, obviously knowing that they will kill each other to possess it. In *Macbeth*, an old man underlines the unnaturalness of Duncan's murder by recounting strange omens that he has not seen before in his seventy years, and he gives God's blessing to 'those that would make good of bad, and friends of foes'.

Marlowe's Old Man appears after Wagner has told the audience that Faustus is near death. At first he is compassionate, encouraging Faustus to repent, but he then turns angry and accusatory, exhorting Faustus to beg mercy from Christ. Unlike the Good Angel, the Old Man is human and therefore cannot be interpreted as a dramatisation of Faustus's conscience. However, his message is the same as the Angel's, trying to reassure Faustus that it is not too late to repent. Being near death himself, he serves as a *memento mori*, a traditional reminder of the inevitability of death and so of the need for repentance. He reminds Faustus that there are no guarantees; he can only find repentance through Christ.

He pushes Faustus to the brink of repentance and Faustus's fate really seems to be in the balance. The Old Man is able to dissuade Faustus from suicide, but knows that Faustus will weaken once he leaves. When the Old Man leaves the stage, Mephistopheles' influence is more powerful, and Faustus irrevocably chooses Hell, spitefully asking his companion to torture the Old Man. This is the point at which the audience realises that Faustus will not be saved. The Old Man returns to the stage while Faustus is embracing Helen, and his silent presence reminds the audience that Faustus has given up his last chance of salvation, just in case we were tempted to allow ourselves to be intoxicated by Marlowe's 'heavenly verse'. The Old Man dies happy, in spite of the tortures being inflicted on him, demonstrating that the powers of Hell can do little against a strong faith. Marlowe uses his end as a contrast with Faustus's end in the following scene.

Helen

Helen does not appear in her 'true substantial' body, but is, in fact, a spirit who 'resembles' the beautiful woman who was the cause of the Trojan War. Helen of Troy was a daughter of Zeus. She was married to Menelaus, king of Sparta, but Paris, a Trojan prince, had been promised Helen by Aphrodite, and he abducted her. After a war that lasted for ten years, Menelaus took Helen back to Sparta. Here, she is an illusion, prepared by the forces of Hell, a succubus who sucks forth Faustus's soul, but she is described in words with Christian associations. One scholar refers to her 'heavenly beauty'; Faustus calls her 'heavenly Helen' and, after kissing the demon in disguise, declares that 'heaven be in these lips'.

In Marlowe's source, Helen is described in minute detail, including her 'roling hawke's eye' and 'smiling and wanton countenance'. The *Faustbuch* reports that Helen bore Faustus a child that disappeared along with its mother on the day of Faustus's death. Marlowe, however, gives no detailed physical description of Helen. When '*music sounds*' and '*Helen, (led in by Mephistopheles,) passeth over the stage*', an impression of her exceptional beauty is conveyed in the awe with which the Scholars speak of her in abstract terms. She is one 'Whom all the world admires for majesty'; her 'heavenly beauty passeth all compare'. She is 'the pride of nature's works/ And only paragon of excellence'. Faustus's longing for her is not, however, ethereal but physical. He thinks that to possess her will 'glut the longing' of his heart's desire, that her 'sweet embracings' will extinguish the thoughts of repentance that keep haunting him. His language here reminds us of his request to Lucifer to let him 'live in all voluptuousness', and her kiss briefly deludes him that he will have a future in which he will relive the past.

Obviously in Marlowe's time Helen would have been played by a boy or a man, and it is through Marlowe's poetry that the illusion of a beautiful woman is created. In the RSC 1974 production, Faustus carried a beautiful mask draped in flowing chiffon across the stage to his bed, which Sir Ian McKellen interprets as 'a cunning revelation of the deceitful nature of the devilish delights which entrance the poor sexually frustrated academic'. It could be argued that Faustus asks for Helen knowing that demoniality, bodily intercourse with spirits, is the ultimate sin, and that he will not be tempted by thoughts of repentance after kissing her. However he might just be seeking diversion again because he is feeling despair.

Faustus: 'this learned man'

Marlowe's play developed out of the morality plays when the central protagonist represented 'mankind' or 'everyman' and was named accordingly. Faustus, however, is more than a mere representative of the human race; he is a fully rounded character in his own right and is a mass of contradictions.

Contradictions

There is plenty of evidence of his intelligence. The Prologue tells us that, 'shortly he was graced with doctor's name,/ Excelling all…' Valdes tells Faustus that he and Cornelius need his 'wit' so that all nations will canonise them. Even the Epilogue speaks of 'Apollo's laurel bough/ That sometime grew within this learned man'. Nevertheless, at times he seems very foolish. He claims that, 'A sound magician is a mighty god' (1.1.64) and dismisses 'these vain trifles of men's souls' (1.3.62). In spite of Mephistopheles's honesty, Faustus still expects the demon to obey him: 'Villain, have I not bound thee to tell me anything?' (2.3.69). He even seems to

think that the succubus who appears in the shape of Helen of Troy will give him his soul back (5.1.93–94).

He seems very courageous in conjuring a spirit, even though he thinks he might die because of it (1.1.168), and in hazarding his immortal soul for knowledge. He scoffs at Mephistopheles's terror, saying 'Learn thou of Faustus manly fortitude,/ And scorn those joys thou never shalt possess' (1.3.86–87). However, when faced with the prospect of his body being tortured by devils, he is a coward and begs forgiveness of Lucifer (5.1.68–70).

At the beginning of the play, he is very arrogant, claiming to have mastered the art of logic (1.1.10–11) and calling himself 'conjuror laureate' (1.3.32). He presumes to know that God does not love him (2.1.9), and, a few lines further on, he claims, 'What god can hurt thee, Faustus? Thou art safe' (2.1.25). However, he learns humility, realising that 'What art thou, Faustus, but a man condemned to die?' (4.1.126). When he is performing tricks for the Emperor and the Duke and Duchess, his gratitude and humility seem excessive.

Faustus seems to need company; he loves debating with anyone — pastors of the Church, scholars and Mephistopheles — and he spends his last evening banqueting with a group of students. However, he is a very solitary person, choosing to conjure alone, even though Cornelius and Valdes wish to work with him. Socially he seems to be quite inept as he seeks Mephistopheles's help to get a wife, and he does not seem to have any friends of his own age and status with whom to spend his last evening on earth. The only person to whom he can bequeath his possessions is his servant.

He has a commendable generosity of spirit, warning the Scholars to leave him in case they perish with him (5.2.44–46), and yet he is extremely spiteful to the Old Man, asking Mephistopheles, 'Torment, sweet friend, that base and crooked age/ That durst dissuade me from thy Lucifer,/ With greatest torments that our hell affords' (5.1.75–77).

It seems that the reason he does not repent is that he is a man of honour, saying 'Hell calls for right...Faustus will come to do thee right' (5.1.49–51). He is honest with the Emperor, admitting that he cannot produce the actual bodies of Alexander and his paramour, only 'such spirits as can lively resemble' them. However, when he is depressed, he blames others for his mistakes. Although Mephistopheles tried to warn him against his course of action, Faustus curses 'wicked Mephistopheles,/ Because thou hast deprived me of those joys' (2.3.2–3). In his final soliloquy, he even curses his parents (5.2.105).

Faustus's likes and dislikes

As well as debating and taking risks, Faustus enjoys new and interesting things and experiences (1.1.86–87), and he finds 'delight' in travel (3.1.2; 3.1.47–48). He loves to hear Homer singing tragic love stories (2.3.26–27) and listening to beautiful

music (2.3.28–30). He is not enthusiastic about playing tricks on the Pope, merely telling Mephistopheles that he is 'content' (3.1.54), and he uses the same adjective to the Emperor (4.1.14); however, he takes 'pleasure' in the 'rarest things and royal courts of kings' (Act 4 Chorus). He is mesmerised by Helen as the epitome of female beauty, telling Mephistopheles that to possess her will 'glut the longing of my heart's desire' (5.1.90–91).

We learn that Faustus dislikes those areas of study which give him no opportunity to show off his cleverness, learn something new or to exercise his intelligence (1.1.106–10). He clearly disliked having had to wear plain clothes when he was a student (1.1.92–93), and he plays a cruel trick on the Knight and warns him to 'hereafter speak well of scholars' (4.1.86).

Different interpretations

There are some points in the play where Faustus's reactions are open to interpretation.

He says that the sight of the Seven Deadly Sins delights his soul (2.3.157), but, when Lucifer and Beelzebub first appear, Faustus asks 'O, who art thou that look'st so terrible?' (2.3.85), so perhaps he is terrified of upsetting Lucifer.

Mephistopheles tells the Horse-courser that Faustus 'has not slept these eight nights' (4.1.151), and there are various possible explanations for this. His time is running out (4.1.92–95) and so he might not wish to waste it in sleep. He might be trying to decide whether to repent or not, or it might be fear of eternal damnation which keeps him awake. He might be spending his nights regretting what he did in his youth.

Similarly, when Wagner tells us that he would have thought that Faustus would not 'banquet and carouse and swill/ Amongst the students' (5.1.4–5) on his last evening on earth, there are several possible explanations for this behaviour. He might still believe that Hell is a **fable** (2.1.127), and so he is safe from damnation. He might still believe in last-minute repentance (4.1.130), or he might be bravely showing 'manly fortitude (1.3.86). Equally, he might be indulging in a 'sweet pleasure' 'to conquer deep despair' (2.3.25).

In the final scene, Marlowe gives Faustus the exclamation 'Ah, Mephistopheles!' Perhaps he is pleased to see the one who has been his constant companion for 24 years, or he might be speaking in an accusing tone, blaming Mephistopheles for his plight. He might be being reminded of something he is trying to forget, or he might be speaking fatalistically, resigned to his fate. He might even be appealing for help.

Renaissance man

As well as making Faustus a flawed individual, Marlowe also gave him the enquiring mind and aspiring spirit of a Renaissance man. As we listen to his speeches, we learn that he seeks wealth (1.1.14; 1.1.55; 1.1.84–85; 2.1.22), as well as fame in posterity and honour in his lifetime (1.1.15; 1.1.56). He also aspires to omnipotence, like a deity (1.1.56; 1.1.64–65), and he specifies what kinds of power he seeks. He desires power over life and death (1.1.24–25), power over the elements and the universe (1.1.58–59; 1.1.91; 1.3.105–09; 1.3.38–39), power over spirits (1.1.81; 2.1.164–66; 1.3.36–37; 1.3.94–98; 2.1.98–104), and, on a more mundane level, military and political power (1.1.94–99; 1.3.105–12; 2.1.23). Above all, he seeks knowledge (1.1.82; 1.1.88–89; 2.1.168–70; 2.1.116–17; 2.1.172–74; 2.3.35–37; 2.3.44; 2.3.55–65; Act 3 Chorus).

Gains and losses

From his pact with Lucifer, Faustus gains the ability to conjure the most renowned poets and musicians to entertain him (2.3.26–30). He is given the opportunity to test his knowledge by flying around in a chariot drawn by dragons (Act 3 Chorus). A succubus, or female demon, in the likeness of Helen of Troy becomes his 'paramour' (5.1). He has the ability to do wonders which all the known world has witnessed (5.2.19–20), but, in his final scene, Faustus realises that all these gains are worthless and he calls them 'The vain pleasure of four and twenty years' (5.2.35–36).

His 24 years, however, have not been totally pleasurable. He complains that 'Scarce can I name salvation, faith, or heaven / But fearful echoes thunders in mine ears:/ 'Faustus, thou art damned!' (2.3.19–21) and weapons are given to him so that he can commit suicide. Next time he calls on Christ (2.3.81), a terrifying Lucifer appears with Beelzebub to frighten him into submission. He has a 'distressèd soul' (5.1.58) and suffers from the recurring despair that comes from a lack of faith in his ability to repent. Eventually he realises that he has lost 'both Germany and the world, yea, heaven itself' (5.2.21), and any chance of 'eternal joy and felicity' (5.2.36–37).

Deep despair and manic recklessness

The psychiatrist Derek Russell Davies cites Faustus as a model for functional psychosis of manic-depressive type, swinging between deep despair and manic reck-lessness. In his soliloquy at the beginning of Act 2, for instance, he despairingly says, 'Now, Faustus, must thou needs be damned,/ And canst thou not be saved', then, believing himself beyond pardon, his mood swings, and he offers to sacrifice new-born babies to Beelzebub.

While signing the contract, he hallucinates, twice seeing writing on his arm: '*Homo fuge!*' Mephistopheles distracts him with devils, and then he wildly declares, 'Then there's enough for a thousand souls.' Another time when he speaks of his despair, he admits that 'long ere this I should have slain myself,/ Had not sweet pleasure conquered deep despair' (2.3.24–25). However, the memory of the beautiful music that he conjures to dispel his depression makes him declare that 'Faustus shall ne'er repent'. Later in the same scene, he miserably tells

Mephistopheles, 'Ay, go, accursèd spirit, to ugly hell!/ 'Tis thou hast damned distressed Faustus' soul' (2.3.74–75). However, after Lucifer shows him the sins, he expresses a reckless desire to see Hell.

After the Old Man admonishes him, Faustus asks 'Where art thou Faustus? Wretch, what hast thou done?/ Damned art thou, Faustus, damned! Despair and die!' (5.1.47–48). However, instead of trying to repent, he asks for Helen as his 'paramour', knowing that bodily contact with a spirit will place him beyond pardon. He deludes himself that a second kiss will return his soul. Despairing because he only has one hour left before he 'must be damned perpetually' (5.2.59), Faustus makes a last desperate bid for the annihilation of his soul in an attempt to avoid his punishment.

Youth

In the final scene, Faustus tells the scholars he has been at Wittenberg for 30 years, which means that he had only been there six years when he signed the contract. Fourteen was the minimum age for admission to Cambridge University, so it is reasonable to assume that, at the beginning of the play, Faustus is in his early twenties. Faustus has devoted himself to his studies and already achieved outstanding successes, not only a Doctorate in Divinity but also a considerable reputation for protecting whole cities from the plague and easing a thousand desperate maladies. Perhaps it is not surprising that these early triumphs have gone to his head. However, he has reached the point where his studies have nothing more to offer him. He could settle down and heap up gold as a doctor, but he wants to achieve miracles (1.1.9), to 'make men live eternally,/ Or, being dead, raise them to life again' (1.1.24–5). Orthodox study offers him everlasting joy in Heaven, but no challenge for a young man with a restless craving for a life of 'profit and delight, of power, of honour, of omnipotence' (1.1.55–56). Like many intelligent young men, he is ambitious, a rebel against authority and not very good at listening to advice.

Mephistopheles: 'sweet friend' or 'accursed spirit'?

Marlowe's source, the English translation of the *Faustbuch*, describes the scene when Faustus conjured Mephistopheles. In a thick wood near Wittenberg, there was a tremendous noise of thunder, lightning and wind:

> whereat suddenly, over his head hung hovering in the air a mighty dragon; then calls Faustus again after his devilish manner, at which there was a monstrous cry in the wood, as if hell had been open, and all the tormented souls cursing their condition. Presently, not three fathom above his head, fell a flame in manner of lightning, and changed itself into a globe.

Eventually, this flame took on the shape of a man. However, Marlowe's stage directions are minimal, so this scene is open to interpretation. A film director could adhere closely to the description in the *Faustbuch*, but on stage it is more difficult. The B-text specifies that Mephistopheles appears as a dragon, and there is a dragon outside the circle on the title page of the 1624 edition.

Marlowe's audience would have believed in devils and the possibility of summoning them. The conjuring scene would have built up their expectations so that they might even have expected to see a real devil, conjured up by the actor. This moment is the climax of a tense, even horrific, scene and Mephistopheles should not disappoint.

True friend

The character of Mephistopheles has been developed out of the Tempter in the morality plays. However, Marlowe has made him more complicated than that. He also seems to emerge as a truthful friend to Faustus. When he first arrives, Mephistopheles sets the limits of Faustus's ability to command him, and he warns that he cannot do anything without Lucifer's permission. This also warns Faustus that, if he follows Lucifer, he will not be free either.

Mephistopheles admits that he came of his own accord, not because Faustus has the power to control him, and he also admits that Lucifer was banished from Heaven for 'aspiring pride and insolence'. He warns Faustus to leave these 'frivolous demands' and reveals his own 'terror' to try to warn Faustus not to follow him into damnation.

After he returns from Lucifer, Mephistopheles tells Faustus that, as with ambitious earthly monarchs, Lucifer's aim is territorial expansion, and warns Faustus that he will get more than he bargained for. Even after Faustus signs the contract, Mephistopheles is truthful about Hell and about his fate as one of the damned, warning that Faustus will learn that Mephistopheles is speaking the truth. He tells Faustus that Lucifer was beautiful before his fall and is no longer. Devils were perceived as ugly because they were immoral, full of sin. He offers himself as evidence that Hell does exist. When Faustus asks for a wife, Mephistopheles cannot oblige because in the sixteenth century there were no civil marriages, so the word 'wife' carried with it associations of the Church and holy matrimony. He could be warning Faustus that he will be denied the blessing of a lifetime companion and only have superficial relationships with prostitutes.

Once Faustus has signed the contract, Mephistopheles is no longer his truthful friend; he lies about Heaven and fetches reinforcements when Faustus thinks of repenting. During the 24 years that he is Faustus's companion, Mephistopheles seems to distract him from his lofty aspirations. Instead of encouraging Faustus's longing to see Rome, as a friend would, Mephistopheles leads him into damning himself further by stealing from God's representative, although it could be argued that, like a friend, he encourages Faustus to lighten up and have fun. Mephistopheles even tries to protect Faustus from the belligerent horse dealer, and he seems sympathetic to Faustus because 'he has not slept these eight nights'.

In the final Act, Mephistopheles is still truthful, admitting that he cannot touch the soul of the faithful Old Man, only hurt his body. Even at this late hour, this should have warned Faustus that, if he turned to God and had faith in God's mercy, the forces of Hell would not be able to do more than 'afflict his body'.

Tempter

Mephistopheles does not act as a tempter until he returns from arranging the terms of the contract with Lucifer in Act 2. He knows that God's mercy is infinite and Faustus's contract with Lucifer is powerless, so he makes Faustus write a deed of gift in his own blood knowing that he will feel bound to his promise. Then he tempts Faustus with 'then be thou as great as Lucifer', but this is a power which he has already explained that he will not have. Like Mephistopheles, Faustus will just be a servant to Lucifer, not 'as great as Lucifer'. When Faustus's blood congeals, Mephistopheles brings unearthly fire to make it flow, and tells the audience in an aside: 'O what will not I do to obtain his soul' (2.1.73).

When Faustus receives a divine message, '*Homo fuge*', Mephistopheles distracts him from repentance and demonstrates powers Faustus will have. He tempts Faustus with political power, symbolised by crowns, and wealth and luxury, symbolised by rich apparel. When Faustus asks for a wife, Mephistopheles punishes him, because marriage was an institution blessed by God. Also, a wife would try to save him, so Faustus must be kept isolated. He tempts Faustus with the offer of a succession of women for his bed, whether he wants them chaste, wise or beautiful. He gives Faustus a book of spells to control the weather and to bring him wealth and military power. Knowing Faustus's thirst for knowledge, Mephistopheles gives him a book that explains the universe.

Mephistopheles tries to reassure Faustus that Heaven is not 'such a glorious thing' as he imagines, which directly contradicts what he has already said (1.3.79–81), so he is lying to prevent Faustus from repenting. When Faustus's resolve falters, and he starts to wonder whether it is too late to repent, Mephistopheles fetches Lucifer and Beelzebub.

Although Faustus wants to learn by experience, and he asks to see Rome, Mephistopheles distracts him by suggesting some fun at the Pope's expense. Mephistopheles is subtly corrupting Faustus's finer feelings. This trivial behaviour demonstrates to Faustus that the Church has no power over him, because he is already damned. It also helps to make him think that he has gone too far for God to forgive him. It is Mephistopheles who instigates the puerile trick on the Horse-courser, further debasing Faustus's lofty ambitions.

When Faustus despairs in the final act, Mephistopheles gives him a dagger, hoping that he will kill himself and so put himself beyond hope of salvation.

Self-murder is the ultimate sin because it is for God to decide when a life comes to an end, and, if Faustus succumbs to despair, it is evident that he does not believe in redemption. When the Old Man tries to persuade Faustus to repent, Mephistopheles does what he can to prevent him from turning back. However, all he can do is accuse Faustus of treachery and disobedience, and threaten to tear his flesh to pieces. Faustus knows that he is destined for an eternity of pain, so the latter is a very weak threat. More powerful is the accusation of treachery because Faustus is an honourable man and will not break his promise. 'Hell calls for right', and the right thing, by Faustus's code of conduct, is to adhere to his contract. Finally, when Faustus asks for Helen of Troy, Mephistopheles brings a devil in the form of Helen 'in the twinkling of an eye', before Faustus can change his mind, knowing that, after bodily intercourse with a spirit (demoniality) there can be no forgiveness.

Mephistopheles is a truthful friend, until Faustus sends him back to Lucifer to arrange the pact. He tries hard to dissuade Faustus until it becomes obvious that he is determined to pursue his course. Once he returns from Lucifer, his truthfulness has a sarcastic edge: 'I will be thy slave and wait on thee,/ And give thee more than thou hast wit to ask', and he begins to fulfil the role of the tempter. Mephistopheles has to be contradictory because Faustus will only put himself at risk if the tempter is good company, someone he would choose as a friend. While seeming to warn Faustus, Mephistopheles gives the seductively false impression that things cannot be that bad in Hell.

Tragic figure

In the sixteenth century, a tragic figure was always someone of consequence who had been led into catastrophe by a fatal flaw or error of judgement. The tragic effect usually depends on an awareness of admirable qualities that are wasted, and the loss being greater than the misjudgement seems to merit. There is plenty of evidence that Marlowe intended Mephistopheles to be a tragic figure in his own right.

Mephistopheles was an angel, living in Heaven in the sight of God, and he has lost everything because he allied himself with Lucifer. An eternity of suffering seems disproportionate for this error of judgement. In a melancholy epistrophe (1.3.71–73), which echoes Faustus's previous line, Mephistopheles admits to being unhappy, acknowledges his crime against 'our God', and laments that his suffering will last 'for ever'. Laden with suppressed anguish, he understands what he has lost, and unselfishly tries to prevent another from making the same mistake.

Mephistopheles warns Faustus not to think of Hell as a place; Hell is being deprived of Heaven and the sight of God. Even a devil feels 'terror' at the thought of what he has done and his soul is 'fainting'. He feels compassion and admits his own misery in an overt attempt to save Faustus. Mephistopheles even admits in a Latin quotation (2.1.42) that he is wretched and wants others to share his misery.

It is his awareness that he is responsible for his own fate as well as his frustration that Faustus is too arrogant to listen to his warnings that make him seem more human than demonic. In 2.1.121–27, he laments his fate once again. He and the other fallen angels will be tortured for eternity; wherever they go they will be in Hell. He no longer tries to dissuade Faustus but is resigned to the fact that Faustus will not learn except by experience.

Acting the part

In several scenes Mephistopheles is on stage but says little, so the actor needs to think very carefully about how he will act when not speaking. He must never upstage Faustus, but he needs to be a compelling presence on stage that the audience is always aware of. If he is an attractive character, witty, ironic and good-humoured, then the audience will keep an eye on him even when he is not speaking. One alternative interpretation was to portray him as a waiting, watching devil. The actor stood very still, never looking directly at Faustus, and was a sad presence, aware of his own tragic mistakes.

Theme I: magic and the supernatural

Magic on stage

In *Doctor Faustus* there are many supernatural characters who actually appear on stage. As well as the Good and Evil Angels, Mephistopheles, Lucifer and Beelzebub, there are the Seven Deadly Sins, various unnamed devils, as well as Balioll and Belcher. There is a succubus who resembles Helen of Troy as well as spirits that resemble Alexander and his paramour. Magic undoubtedly gives the play that frisson of fear that has always delighted theatre audiences. Indulging in forbidden acts on stage holds the potential for the unknown and unexpected to happen, and the play is probably most successful when the production takes advantage of opportunities for spectacular theatrical effects.

Marlowe's company would have used frightening costumes for Mephistopheles's first appearance, and for Lucifer, Beelzebub and the minor devils. Fireworks sometimes accompany the devils. There would have been comic costumes for the Seven Deadly Sins, and elaborate costumes for those actors pretending to be spirits who resemble historical characters. The magic invisibility robe that Faustus wears to play tricks on the Pope requires suspension of disbelief by the audience. Human beings are turned into animals, and this could be achieved using body language and costume; the Knight appears with a pair of horns on his head, and there is a farcical scene in which Faustus loses a leg.

Some magical occurrences are only described because they could not be reproduced on the Elizabethan stage. In Chorus 3, Wagner narrates how Faustus 'did mount himself to scale Olympus' top'. Olympus is a real mountain, but it was thought to be the home of the Olympian Gods in ancient Greece, so perhaps Marlowe is suggesting that he could travel through time as well as space. Wagner also tells that he travelled 'seated in a chariot burning bright/ Drawn by the strength of yoky dragons' necks'. At times, Faustus has supernatural experiences that the audience would not be able to see. These raise the possibility that they are hallucinations and the whole story is happening inside his head, which is an idea that John Barton explored in the 1974 production by the RSC. As he tries to sign the contract, his blood congeals but then starts to flow again when Mephostopheles applies a chafer of coals. Earthly fire would not have this effect so it must be some kind of supernatural fire. Immediately after this, he sees the Latin phrase '*homo fuge*' inscribed on his arm. It disappears and then returns.

In his final soliloquy, Faustus is aware of something or somebody pulling him down when he tries to leap up to God, and then he feels as if his heart is being torn because he has spoken Christ's name. He sees 'Christ's blood' stream in the firmament, God stretching out His arm and bending 'his ireful brows', then later he sees God looking fiercely down on him.

Renaissance magic

When Faustus spurns the traditional academic disciplines of Analytics and Philosophy, Medicine, the Law and Divinity, he also rejects all the conventional authorities of Aristotle, Galen, Justinian and the Bible because they imposed limitations on him. He turns to the 'metaphysics of magicians' and 'necromantic books', thinking that, through them, he will achieve aspirations which have no limits but stretch 'as far as doth the mind of man'. The Renaissance was an exciting time of change and upheaval in almost every walk of life, and magic allows Marlowe to draw together many of the aspirations of Renaissance thinkers. Faustus, Cornelius and Valdes believed that magic could help them to achieve the enjoyment of worldly beauty and the indulgence of the senses. They sought dominion over the universe, wealth and political power, as well as infinite knowledge.

Cornelius and Valdes

The evidence suggests that, although one of the orthodox Scholars says that Cornelius and Valdes are infamous throughout the world for 'that damned art', they practise benevolent or 'white' magic. They seek knowledge of astrology, which consists of interpreting the influence of stars and planets on earthly affairs and human destinies. At the time, astrology was inseparable from astronomy. They seek knowledge about the mystical properties of minerals, which are thought to have therapeutic powers. They also want knowledge of languages. Greek and Hebrew were desirable for those who would converse with spirits, but Latin was the recognised common tongue. Dee and his assistant, Edward Kelly, conjured up and talked to a variety of apparitions, mostly good angels but some evil spirits, and they held angelic conversations in a mixture of these languages and an unintelligible spirit language known as 'Enochian'.

The writings Cornelius and Valdes rely on in their study of magic are all written by devout men. They study the writings of Roger Bacon, a deeply religious philosophy teacher at Oxford University in the thirteenth century who identified a distinction between legitimate, benevolent magic and the 'damnable invocation of demons'. They also study 'Albanus', who is generally thought to be Pietro d'Abano, the pious medieval Italian philosopher, astrologer and professor of medicine at Padua University, who endeavoured to account for the wonderful effects in nature by the influence of the celestial bodies rather than accepting orthodox doctrine which attributed them to angels or demons. For their incantation, they need 'the Hebrew Psalter', especially Psalms 22 and 51, and lastly they need the New Testament, probably the opening words of St John's Gospel: 'In the beginning was the Word, and the Word was with God, and the Word was God.'

Faustus

If we look closely at the scene in which Faustus conjures Mephistopheles (1.3), we can see that Cornelius and Valdes do not appear to have had much influence on him. Whereas Cornelius and Valdes talk of conjuring 'the subjects of every element', Faustus starts his conjuring by saying 'Faustus, begin thine incantations,/ And try if devils will obey thy hest.' Faustus does not use any phrases from the Psalms or from the New Testament. He does conjure in Latin and command the subjects of the elements to appear by invoking the name of Jehovah, sprinkling holy water, and making the sign of the cross, but he does not persevere in this vein.

When he fails to conjure the spirits of the elements immediately, he appeals to Lucifer and Beelzebub that Mephistopheles, another of the angels thrown out of Heaven, should appear. When still nothing happens, being impatient, he then performs actions to renounce his Christian baptism by misusing the baptismal water and forswearing the vows made at his christening. It is significant that Mephistopheles explains that Faustus did not conjure him; he came of his own accord because Faustus violated the name of God and formally rejected the Scriptures. It seems that Faustus was too impatient to work with Cornelius and Valdes to conjure spirits by legitimate means, and he took a fatal short-cut.

Theme II: condemnation or celebration?

As we have seen, identifying the conflicts in a play leads us to an awareness of the wider themes with which the play is concerned. There seems to be a conflict in the genre of *Doctor Faustus* so that it is unclear whether it is a morality play or a tragedy in which the protagonist's fatal flaw is intellectual curiosity.

Morality play

As in a morality play, the central character is 'base of stock', and so he seems to represent humanity. Faustus meets a succession of figures of temptation, figures who represent the Seven Deadly Sins and even Lucifer himself. He gives in to temptation, realises his mistake and succumbs to despair. He is invited to commit suicide and so put himself beyond redemption. Redemption is offered by the Good Angel and the Old Man, reinforcing a clear moral message that celebrates the Christian belief that sinners may be saved through Christ's mercy. Faustus is punished for his disobedience and presumption by being taken to Hell through a gaping mouth which is one of the props used in morality plays, graphically symbolising pain and punishment. There are several scenes of low comedy, knockabout **farce** and bawdy word play. The audience is warned at the beginning and at the end not to follow Faustus's example.

However, the play differs from a conventional morality play in several significant ways. The Chorus, a device from Greek drama, tells the audience that Faustus was not innocent at the start of the play; he is already 'swoll'n with cunning' and already 'surfeits upon cursed necromancy'. Unlike Everyman or Mankind, Faustus is exceptionally clever and has been awarded a doctorate in Divinity. Furthermore, he does not manage to repent because he believes the contract he signed is binding and it is too late. Faustus is tempted by his own desire for knowledge and power, rather than by other characters. He tells Cornelius and Valdes that it is 'not your words only, but mine own fantasy' which have led to his decision. He uses them to achieve his ends. He conjures Mephistopheles and, until he signs the contract, the fallen angel tries to dissuade him. Neither Faustus nor Mephistopheles is the two-dimensional cipher of morality plays. Both are detailed and complex creations.

Marlowe's plays are a new form of tragedy, based on Greek drama and focusing on an individual. Rather than showing mankind's place in the cosmos as an **allegory** does, a tragedy shows an individual challenging the order of the cosmos. Whereas morality plays showed man to be frail, subject to temptation, but redeemable through God, Marlowe shows a human with the self-belief to defy God. Although Faustus is destroyed, we have been encouraged to sympathise with him.

Renaissance tragedy

The sixteenth century inherited from the medieval world a system of beliefs that held that everything in the universe had its set place. Man's place was lowly; full of sin, he must suffer in this world in the hope of salvation. However, in the Renaissance this was questioned. The medieval ideal of a life of contemplation was rejected for a life of action and achievement. Faustus embodies the new enquiring and aspiring spirit of the age of the Renaissance because he is a free thinker, challenging the teachings of the Church. He believes 'hell's a fable' (2.1.127), and religion is designed, as Machiavelli had said, to keep men in their place. Christianity is based on the premise that the reward of sin is death, but, if we confess and repent, Christ will forgive and cleanse us. Faustus says 'I do repent and yet I do despair./ Hell strives with grace for conquest in my breast' (5.1.63–64). The psychomachia, or struggle for his soul, goes on inside his mind throughout the play, and he is unable to repent because he just is not sure whether Christ will save him.

Faustus is an empiricist, determined to believe only what he can prove. He is dissatisfied with conventional branches of learning because he has learnt everything the university can teach, 'Yet art thou still but Faustus and a man'. His excitement at the thought of acquiring riches and delicacies from around the world reflects the excitement felt by Queen Elizabeth and her subjects for the stories and wonders brought back by explorers such as Sir Walter Raleigh and Sir Francis Drake. He longs to be resolved 'of all ambiguities' (1.1.82) and to learn 'strange philosophy' (1.1.88). The first thing he asks Mephistopheles for is knowledge about Hell (2.1.116–17). Like the humanists, he is questioning the Church's teaching. After asking for a wife, he then wants to learn to raise up spirits. Like God who has angels to do his bidding, Faustus wants spirits to help him achieve his aims.

Memorable passages

There are some passages that convey Faustus's excitement at the possibilities offered by magic. In the first two lines of 1.1.55–65, the list of five abstract nouns builds up in intensity to the Latinate and polysyllabic climax of the divine quality of 'omnipotence', as Faustus is carried away by the excitement of his dreams. The forward movement of this list obscures the line division, and four of the following lines are run on to allow Faustus to enthuse about the limitless possibilities of magic, without interruption.

This passage is a superb description of the Renaissance mind and the belief that the possibilities open to man are only limited by the human imagination; the 'dominion' to which Faustus aspires 'stretcheth as far as does the mind of man', but this is only open to the man who 'exceeds' in this study. Faustus loves to be hyperbolic so it is not enough to excel, he must 'exceed'. The evocative word 'god'

is placed at the end of a line and of a sentence as he wonders at this mind-numbing possibility. The last line of this soliloquy reveals Faustus to be a gambler, hazarding not his life but his mind in the hope that he may 'gain a deity'.

Lines 1.1.84–86 give examples of the 'desperate enterprise(s)' he talks of in the previous lines; the concrete examples are more memorable than the abstract possibilities first considered. Enthusiastically, Faustus's tongue dwells on the final long syllables of the lines and their rich possibilities, 'gold', 'pearls' and 'world'. 'Ransack' is at the beginning of a line and reads most comfortably with two stressed syllables as it conveys the impression of a frenzied search. The polysyllabic 'India' and 'orient', referring as they do to places which Marlowe's audience could only imagine, allow the actor to savour the words and the idea of what they represent.

The most famous speech of the play (5.1.90–109) is spoken after the Old Man's visit has led Faustus to the brink of repentance, and he has asked Mephistopheles for Helen as his 'paramour'. This time he does not just want a vision, he desires a 'woman' to whom he can make love, so that his thoughts of repentance are finally extinguished. He knows that bodily intercourse with a spirit will put him beyond redemption and stop the tormenting psychomachia in which the forces of good and evil battle for his soul. Suicide would have the same result, but how much more haunting is this evocation of beauty. The soaring lyricism of this speech has a poignant undercurrent that makes it more memorable than most poems to a beautiful woman and more memorable than the Chorus's didactic warnings to the audience.

We are given no physical description of Helen, but Marlowe includes memorable images of the vast Greek army launched to reclaim her and the burning of the city of Troy with its 'topless towers', symbols of limitless aspiration that reach straight up into the clouds. Faustus proposes to re-enact the Trojan War through the sack of Wittenberg, but he imagines himself as Paris, vainly battling for the woman he loves, reminding the audience that he is putting himself beyond salvation.

Faustus employs the magic of language to erase thoughts of his peril, but the words and images he uses reveal that he is still dwelling on it. He knows that the succubus's lips really do suck forth his soul, but seems to delude himself that he can get it back. The only 'heaven' he will know is in Helen's lips. His imagery is a reminder that Helen's is a beauty that leads to destruction, like the destruction of Semele, who looked on 'flaming Jupiter' and was struck by lightning, and Arethusa, who was loved by Alphaeus and was turned into a spring.

Conclusion

Marlowe started university as a scholar aiming for a career in the Church, and this would have made him part of the establishment. His work as a spy for Sir Francis Walsingham led the university to question his suitability to be awarded the MA, and, although the Queen's Privy Council intervened, he did not take the expected course but went to London and joined the theatrical set, which was on the fringe of respectability. His colourful lifestyle, his careless tongue, and his association with the freethinkers of Raleigh's circle gained him a reputation as an atheist (indeed, throughout the centuries critics have identified him with Faustus). Because of these associations he needed to give the play an explicit rejection of Faustus and his aspirations.

In taking as his hero a man who rejects God, Marlowe is taking a risk that no other playwright of his time dared to do. The framework of a morality play gave Marlowe the freedom to explore unorthodox ideas and at the same time to appease the censor with warnings against the dangers of these potentially attractive strands of thought. All the heresies are spoken by a devil or by a man who is eventually seen to suffer the punishment of eternal damnation.

However, it could be that this **ambiguity** is Marlowe's way of thinking ideas through for himself. He explores the ways in which orthodox teaching can be challenged by someone with an enquiring mind who is prepared to gamble that 'the first beginning of Religion was only to keep men in awe', as Richard Baines, the government informer against Marlowe, reported. He also explores what might happen to this man if he is wrong.

Imagery and symbolism

Heaven

We are not given a clear image of Heaven in this play; Mephistopheles merely says that Heaven is a place of 'eternal joys' and 'everlasting bliss' (1.3.79–81). The Good Angel vaguely urges Faustus to 'think of heaven and heavenly things' (2.1.20), whereas the Old Man imagines 'celestial rest' (5.1.38). Faustus himself imagines it to be 'heaven, the seat of God, the throne of the blessed, the kingdom of joy' (5.2.21–23) and a place of 'eternal joy and felicity' (5.2.36–37). It sounds rather a boring place for a restless man who likes to take risks and confront challenges.

God

Although God is presented as infinitely merciful to those who repent, he is spoken of as an angry god in the play. The Good Angel warns of his 'heavy wrath' (1.1.74). Even before he has signed the contract, Faustus thinks that God will throw him down to Hell if he tries to repent (2.1.78). In his final soliloquy, Faustus declares that he can 'see where God/ Stretcheth out his arm and bends his ireful brows!' (5.2.74–75), and he calls on mountains to fall on him and hide him 'from the heavy wrath of God' (5.2.77). Near his end, he cries out 'My God, my God, look not so fierce on me' (5.2.112). Even the Old Man imagines a sadistic God who would send Satan to torture him in order to test his faith (5.1.114). Like Milton in *Paradise Lost*, the God Marlowe depicts is the vindictive, wrathful God of the Old Testament.

Hell

The references to Hell reflect the contemporary debates. Faustus at first thinks Hell is an imaginary place, a superstition like the Greek underworld (1.3.60). Mephistopheles disabuses him, describing it as a state of mind. It is everywhere that is not Heaven; Hell is being excluded from the eternal joys of Heaven (1.3.77–81; 2.1.121–26). However, he also refers to it as a place 'under the heavens…Within the bowels of these elements,/ Where we are tortured and remain forever' (2.1.118–20).

In view of this contradictory evidence, perhaps it is not surprising that Faustus is confused and continues to think Hell is a 'fable (2.1.127), especially when Mephistopheles is 'Walking, disputing, etc.' (2.1.139). To an academic who loves debate, this must sound more like heaven! When Faustus declares that the pageant of the Seven Deadly Sins feeds his soul, Lucifer tells Faustus that 'in hell is all manner of delight' (2.3.158). Faustus is, understandably, curious and declares a wish to see Hell and return, but this is at the beginning of his 24 years.

As midnight, the time at which Lucifer said he would send for him, approaches, Faustus is no longer so curious to see Hell. Now he sees it as perpetual damnation (5.2.59) and a place where the souls of men will be plagued (5.2.104). It appears that adders and serpents stifle him and he sees 'ugly hell' (5.2.114) gaping like a monstrous mouth before he leaves escorted by devils.

Lucifer

Lucifer was the brightest of all the angels, and God had given him a position of authority in Heaven. He was perfect until 'iniquity' was found in him. God threw him from the face of Heaven because of his 'aspiring pride and insolence' (1.3.68), and Mephistopheles describes him as 'arch-regent and commander of all spirits' (1.3.64). He was the best of all the angels, and so he fell from the highest to the lowest point: '*corruptio optimi pessima est*' ('the corruption of the best becomes the worst').

When Lucifer appears he looks terrifying, but the actor must have relied on his costume and the theatrical effects, because he does not sound terrifying. He is more like an entertainer, providing a diversion to amuse Faustus and distract him from repentance. We can tell that the costumes were elaborate because, before the permanent theatres were built which charged admission, travelling companies used to take a collection at the time when the main devil was due to appear. The actor's horrific costume was obviously an attraction in itself that people would pay extra to see. The most awesome description of Lucifer comes when Mephistopheles calls on him to witness his vexation at Robin and Rafe: 'Monarch of hell, under whose black survey/ Great potentates do kneel with awful fear;/ Upon whose altars thousand souls do lie' (3.2.28–30). However, Mephistopheles later tells Faustus that Lucifer is powerless over strong faith like that of the Old Man (5.1.81).

The elements

Marlowe frequently uses imagery associated with the four elements of medieval science, medicine and philosophy:

Earth

Mephistopheles says that Hell is 'within the bowels of these elements' (2.1.119), deep within the earth. Cornelius needs to be well-grounded in the study of minerals, alchemy, in order to conjure. Mephistopheles is able to conjure up the spirits of people buried in the earth. The earth contains the kingdom of Lucifer; in addition, according to the Bible, God created Adam out of the earth. In his final soliloquy, when Faustus wishes to hide from God, he calls on mountains and hills to fall on him and the earth to gape so that he can run headlong into it.

Air

The soul was thought to be the breath of God. The body dies but the soul lives for ever. God lives in the empyreal Heaven, beyond the firmament. Faustus sees Christ's blood stream in the firmament, but even this sign does not give him the strength to repent. In his last hour of life, Faustus commands the ever-moving spheres of Heaven to stand still in an attempt to freeze time. He prays to the stars whose positions at his birth determined that he would be damned, begging them to suck him up into a dark cloud, as if he were a foggy mist, so that his limbs could be vomited out again in a storm, freeing his soul to ascend to Heaven. He has a desperate hope that he could hide in a storm cloud (5.2.81–87).

Water

The previous image involves water as well as air. Later in the speech Faustus begs for the disintegration of the soul into little water drops so that he can fall into the ocean and be lost forever (5.2.110–11). He hopes to be able to command water, but there is no evidence that he can, although spirits have apparently told Cornelius that they can dry the sea.

Fire

Fire is associated with Hell. In the Book of Revelations, there are four references to Hell as the oxymoronic 'lake of fire' burning with brimstone. The fusing of two elements here symbolises chaos, and the fire symbolises the intellectual pain of the loss of Heaven as well as the physical pain as punishment for wickedness. Mephistopheles brings infernal fire to make Faustus's congealing blood flow freely. Witches and heretics were burned at the stake to give them and the onlookers a taste of hell-fire in the hope that they would repent before they died. Faustus's final attempt to escape punishment is to offer to burn his books. Fire has always been used as a symbol of the destruction of forbidden knowledge; for instance, William Tyndale's translation of the New Testament into English was publicly burned in

1526 and Salman Rushdie's *Satanic Verses* suffered the same fate in 1988. In the Epilogue, the Chorus speaks metaphorically of the burning of the laurel bough which symbolised Faustus's academic excellence, so it seems like a symbolic punishment for his presumption.

Faustus's aspirations

Marlowe uses imagery to explore the aspirations Faustus has for 'a world of profit and delight,/ Of power, of honour, of omnipotence' (1.1.55–56).

Profit

Faustus talks of sending spirits to fetch gold and pearls, but he rejects heaping up gold as a physician as well as the 'external trash' that lawyers can earn. It is not wealth for its own sake he wants, but the excitement of discovery. At the time Marlowe was writing, explorers were bringing back treasures from the new worlds, as well as 'pleasant fruits and princely delicates'.

Delight

Delight is opposed to duty and therefore anathema to Puritans. It is a vague term, dependent on personal preference. If we put here those aspirations that do not fit into the other categories, we find that Faustus expects to find delight in the resolution of 'all ambiguities', 'strange philosophy' and 'the secrets of all foreign kings'. He wants knowledge that is not available to him at the moment. The secrets of kings may sound like petty gossip, but Marlowe is assumed to have been one of Walsingham's spies, in which case he knew the value of secret intelligence.

Power

To symbolise power over the elements, he mentions making the Rhine circle Wittenberg (1.1.91) and joining Africa and Spain (1.3.108–09). To symbolise political power, he desires to be emperor of the world (1.3.105) and to make both Spain (Protestant England's arch-enemy) and Africa (largely unexplored) 'contributory' to his crown (1.3.108–10). He speaks of chasing the 'Prince of Parma' out of the Netherlands (1.1.95). Only the defeat of the Spanish Armada had prevented Parma from invading England in 1588, so this aspiration symbolises military power for the preservation of independence and freedom. Similarly, 'the fiery keel at Antwerp's bridge' helped defeat the Spanish forces besieging Antwerp in 1584.

Honour

To enable the audience to understand what is meant by honour, Marlowe gives Faustus comparisons with Musaeus, a legendary poet who was surrounded by the spirits of priests and bards in the Greek underworld, and with Cornelius Agrippa, the scholar and necromancer 'whose shadows made all Europe honour him' (1.1.117–20).

Omnipotence

The Christian God is omnipotent, omniscient, omnipresent and all-wise, so, if you aspire to become 'a mighty god' (1.1.64), you are challenging Him. Satan challenged God and was cast out of Heaven; Eve took the fruit from the tree of knowledge because 'it was a tree to be desired to make one wise' (Genesis 3:6), and so she and Adam were cast out of Eden. Faustus knows what he is risking.

Valdes and Cornelius

Marlowe also gives Valdes and Cornelius imagery to help convey the exciting possibilities of magic. Valdes conjures images of what explorers had seen on their travels and anticipates making spirits appear like lions, German cavalry, Lapland giants and beautiful women. At their command, the spirits will bring huge treasure ships from Venice and gold from America. He uses a reference to the mythological story of the Golden Fleece sought by Jason and the Argonauts to suggest adventure and excitement as well as wealth.

Cornelius tempts Faustus with honour and renown for his knowledge of astrology and geology, as well as his ability to speak languages. Perhaps Marlowe is thinking here of his well-known contemporary, Dr John Dee, who wrote of conversations with angels held in a mixture of English, Latin, Greek and Enochian, an unintelligible spirit language. He evokes the image of the oracle of Apollo at Delphi to give Faustus an idea of how many people will flock to him because of his great knowledge. He also suggests power over the elements with fanciful images of drying up the sea, so that spirits can salvage the treasure from wrecked ships, and also finding all the treasure buried in the past. Once again it is not the wealth that excites, but the manner of collecting it.

Blood

Blood is a recurring image that quickly achieves symbolic status. When Faustus is convinced that God will not forgive him, he clearly wants to please Satan. He offers to build an altar and a church, blasphemously subverting Christian images for infernal worship. Then, in deep despair, he thinks of what might be the worst crime, the most evil act, he could commit in order to prove his loyalty to Satan — killing a new-born child and catching its blood in a goblet to offer Satan. This blasphemously recalls the Last Supper, when Jesus offered his disciples a goblet of wine saying, 'This is my blood of the new covenant, which is shed for many.' He was invoking God's covenant with Moses, the 'old' covenant: 'For the life of the flesh is in the blood, and I have given it to you upon the altar to make atonement for your souls; for it is the blood that makes atonement for the soul' (Leviticus 17:11). For Christians, God's covenant with Moses is not abolished but is superseded by the 'new' covenant, consecrated by the Son of God. This is symbolically acknowledged in the communion wine.

For Christians, blood symbolises Christ's love for humanity, and through this love (or blood), the promise of eternal life and the resurrection of the body. For Christians, when Christ became human and spilled his blood on the cross, blood became divine; it became spirit, and this transfiguration from the physical to the spiritual was the opening to eternal life in God. Human blood, a symbol of mortality, becomes divine, wholly spiritual, when cleansed from the stain of sin through the offering of Christ's sinless blood. To use this symbolic blood to write a contract offering his soul to Lucifer would make Faustus believe that his blasphemous action has put him beyond the reach of God's mercy. The use of blood symbolises the permanent and supernatural nature of this pact. When his blood congeals, because of the religious symbolism it seems like a warning from God not to continue. At the very least, his own body is rebelling against the unnatural act.

When Marlowe's Old Man says, 'Break heart, drop blood, and mingle it with tears' (5.1.39), he is urging Faustus to repent but warns that his repentance must be accompanied with sacrifice.

When Faustus sees 'where Christ's blood streams in the firmament!' (5.2.70). Marlowe is reminding his audience that Christ's death on the cross is a blood sacrifice to God the Father which atones for the sins of humanity, thus re-establishing the harmony between humanity and God that had been destroyed by sin.

Helen of Troy

On one level, Helen is a diversion to distract Faustus from thoughts of repentance. However, she is not just an image; this, like Alexander, is a spirit which resembles Helen. Faustus warned the Scholars to 'Be silent then, for danger is in words' (5.1.24), but he fails to follow his own advice, uttering the famous speech of admiration and even kissing her, before leaving the stage with her.

Helen represents beauty, but beauty that carries destruction with it. Whether voluntarily or not, Helen left her husband for another man, and in so doing she set in motion a horrific war that lasted for ten years. Faustus must have known that bodily intercourse with a spirit was the one unpardonable offence; perhaps that is why he asked for Helen to be his paramour, to put himself out of reach of the temptation to repent.

All the images in his magnificent speech are images of destruction. The 'thousand ships' were Greek warships, launched to destroy Troy, and 'The topless towers of Ilium' were burned because of her. Faustus talks of sacking Wittenberg, as the Greeks sacked Troy. He refers to Achilles being killed when wounded in his heel, his only weak spot. Semele was destroyed when she looked on Jupiter, because his divine splendour was too much for mortal eyes to bear. Semele is another overreacher or 'forward wit' who, against advice, insisted on looking on her divine lover. Even the nymph Arethusa is an image of destruction because, after exciting the river god's passion while bathing, she was dissolved into water to protect her from him.

The Seven Deadly Sins

The pageant of the Sins is a kind of shorthand. Instead of giving us scene after scene of Faustus succumbing to each of the sins in turn, Marlowe parades the abstract concepts before us as characters to indicate that, during his 24 years of 'voluptuousness', Faustus indulged in a range of experiences that they represent. The Sins that Lucifer shows to Faustus are allegorical figures from the tradition of morality plays. They would have been grotesquely costumed in character and would have been intended to make the audience laugh.

In Christian terms, 'All unrighteousness is sin' (1 John 5:16–17). Sin is transgression of divine law, unlike 'crimes' that transgress man's laws. The Catholic Church divided sin into two principal categories: 'venial', which are relatively minor, and could be forgiven, and the more severe 'mortal' sin. Mortal sins destroy the life of grace, and create the threat of eternal damnation unless either absolved through the sacrament of confession, or forgiven through perfect contrition on the part of the penitent. Each sin was punished by an appropriate punishment in Hell for all eternity.

Pride

Pride was considered to be the most serious of the sins. It is identified as conceit or excessive self-esteem, especially when the proud person does not accept his/her proper position in the Great Chain of Being. Lucifer was evicted from Heaven because he would not accept the Son of God being placed at God's right hand, which he considered to be his rightful place, just as Macbeth would not accept Duncan's elevation of his son, Malcolm, to be the heir to the throne. Those guilty of pride were destined to be broken on the wheel in Hell. In the pageant, Pride is too arrogant to accept the position into which he has been born and he has an inflated idea of his self-worth.

Covetousness (avarice)

Covetousness or avarice is a sin of excess, particularly applied to the acquisition of wealth. Those guilty of avarice were destined to be put into cauldrons of boiling oil. In the pageant, covetousness is presented as a miser.

Wrath

Wrath refers to inordinate and uncontrolled feelings of anger that can lead to such offences as assault and murder. In Marlowe's time, the sin of wrath also encompassed anger turned against oneself, leading to self-harm. Those guilty of wrath were destined to be dismembered alive. In the pageant, Wrath has been angry since birth with no provocation, and he attacks himself when he has no one else to fight.

Envy

Envy is characterised by spite and resentment at seeing the success of another. Those who commit the sin of envy resent the fact that another person has something they

see themselves as lacking and may even gloat if another person loses that something. Those guilty of envy were destined to be put into freezing water. In the pageant, Envy is resentful of anyone who has something he does not, and his resentment prevents him from enjoying what he does have. He wishes to pull everyone else down to his level.

Gluttony

Gluttony is the over-consumption of food and drink to the point of waste. Those guilty of gluttony were destined to be forced to eat rats, toads and snakes. In the pageant, Gluttony over-indulges and is resentful of anyone who does not indulge him.

Sloth

Sloth is idleness, the failure to utilise the talents given to you by God. Those guilty of sloth were destined to be thrown into snake pits. In the pageant, Sloth resents any attempts to make him do anything at all.

Lechery

Lechery or lust refers to excessive and unrestrained indulgence in sexual activity. Sexual intercourse was considered to be purely for the purposes of procreation, so any sexual act that was indulged in for enjoyment rather than to produce children was sinful. Those guilty of lechery were destined to be smothered in fire and brimstone. Lechery is the only one in the pageant who is obviously female. In Elizabethan times it was thought that the Devil targeted men through women who, like Eve, were ruled by their appetites rather than reason, given to delusive imaginings and far too feeble spiritually to resist temptation.

Faustus's sins

Faustus is certainly guilty of pride. The Prologue tells us that he is 'swoll'n with cunning of a self-conceit', and Faustus himself claims to be 'conjurer laureate'. Perhaps more significant is that he is too proud to ask for God's mercy; he presumes to know that God will never forgive him: 'To God? He loves thee not' (2.1.9). Marlowe's language suggests that Faustus is guilty of a metaphorical gluttony as he has stuffed himself full of permitted learning and plans to over-indulge on the forbidden arts. The Prologue uses the metaphor when he says that 'glutted more with learning's golden gifts,/ He surfeits upon cursed necromancy', and Faustus admits to being 'glutted with conceit of this!' (1.1.80). Faustus certainly thinks he is lecherous, saying 'I am wanton and lascivious and cannot live without a wife' (2.1.140–41), and asking for Helen 'To glut the longing of my heart's desire' (5.1.82). However, it might seem to the audience that he is sexually frustrated because he has no experience of women. Faustus corrupts his servant, who in his turn corrupts his servant, so their souls are endangered as well. He also asks Mephistopheles to torture the old Man for trying to persuade Faustus to repent (5.1.77).

Faustus's final soliloquy

Faustus's final soliloquy would make a brilliant audition piece as it really challenges an actor's skills. Faustus explores various strategies to avoid damnation. He attempts to command the universe to cease its motion, and he commands the sun to rise again just after 11 p.m. and to remain risen forever. He tries to extend time so that this one hour becomes long enough for him to repent. He tries to leap up to God, and he calls on Christ to save him. When this fails, he calls on mountains and hills to fall on him and hide him, or he expects the earth to gape so that he can hide deep inside it. He commands the stars to draw him up like a foggy mist. He begs God to set a limit on his pain so he does not suffer for eternity. He hopes to be changed into an animal so he will not have a soul. He looks for someone else to blame. He commands his body to turn to air, and his soul to turn to water. Finally, he offers to burn his books of magic.

Language and imagery

There are some interesting features of language in this speech that are worth exploring. A series of imperatives: 'Stand still', 'rise again', 'come and fall on me', 'gape!', 'draw up', show this once powerful conjuror still trying to issue orders to the universe. In fact, he cannot even command his own body, which does not 'turn to air'. The **dramatic irony** is that we know that his commands will fail, and we know the endings of his two lists: 'A year, a month, a week, a natural day' will be followed logically by an hour, which is what he has. 'Let Faustus live in hell a thousand years,/ A hundred thousand'; the logical end to this progression is infinity.

As Faustus struggles to find escape, he conjures up images of how this might be achieved. From line 60 to 66, Faustus employs imagery of time in order to try to prevent midnight coming or to give him more time to repent. Just as it looks as if he might repent, imagining leaping up to God and seeing Christ's blood streaming in the firmament, his repentance turns into begging Lucifer not to hurt him any more, and he sees the image of angry God, stretching out his arm as if in threat. From line 76 to 87, his imagery is spatial as he explores the possibility that there might be somewhere in the universe where he might be safe. After the clock has struck the half-hour, as Faustus's desperation increases, the imagery he uses tends more towards imagery of dissolution.

Form, structure and time

Underlying the speech is the iambic pentameter of blank verse, but, in order to help the actor to convey the panic of a terrified mind, Marlowe has employed various strategies to break up the rhythm. He has used some short lines and an extra syllable

on line 71. He has also included run-on lines, or enjambement. He has varied the metre by using inverted initial iambic feet on lines 75, 76 and 105, and by putting a spondee, or two heavy stresses, at the beginning of lines 60, 70 and 80. Fifteen of the lines have multiple mid-line caesuras to break up the rhythm. He has also frequently used repetition, exclamations and questions.

The structure of this speech is similar to Faustus's first soliloquy; in both speeches, Faustus is considering a series of options and systematically rejecting them. This structural similarity invites the audience to remember the first scene, when Faustus, a scholar with a glorious future, took the first step that led to this end. Now, however, instead of looking forward with excitement to the future, contemplating a career for life, he is desperately looking for ways to escape everlasting damnation.

Marlowe cleverly manipulates time in this scene. He gives the actor 59 lines to enact an hour of fictional time. Thirty-one lines take us to when the clock strikes the half-hour and then Marlowe creates the illusion of time passing more quickly as Faustus panics because there are only 20 lines until the hour begins to strike. Fictional time is speeded up, and this is the opposite of what Faustus wants. The last eight lines of the speech are given extra intensity as the clock inexorably strikes 12 times.

Stage directions

This is a very dramatic speech, in which Marlowe implicitly suggests actions for the actor. On line 69, Faustus tries to leap up to God, stretching towards Heaven, but something is pulling him down. This image is reflected on the title page of the 1604 edition, where the printer's device shows a boy with wings upon his right arm and with his left hand holding, or fastened to, a weight. On line 70, Faustus points up to the heavens where he can supposedly see Christ's blood streaming, then he appeals to Christ. It might be appropriate if the actor were to fall to his knees at this point as it seems as if he is starting to repent.

On line 72, he clutches his heart, as it feels as if Lucifer is tearing at it, then once again it seems that he looks up to the heavens. First he is puzzled because the vision of Christ's blood has disappeared, and then he sees God angrily looking at him and stretching out His arm. Perhaps the actor might throw himself on the stage in an attempt to hide from God. On line 80, he commands the earth to gape so that he can hide. Perhaps it might be appropriate if the actor pulls vainly at the trapdoor in the stage.

On the striking of the half-hour, Faustus sounds resigned to his fate, saying ''Twill all be past anon.' Then, once again the actor could kneel as he implores God to 'impose some end to (his) incessant pain'. When midnight begins to strike, he panics: 'O, it strikes, it strikes! Now, body, turn to air' (line 108), and once again he looks up to God's face in the heavens.

By line 113, it seems Faustus cannot breathe. He seems to be having hallucinations that adders and serpents are choking him. If so, perhaps the actor could tear
at imaginary things at his throat. On the next line he sees Hell's mouth gaping to
receive him. Perhaps a curtain has been drawn back from the inner stage under the
minstrel's gallery to reveal the mouth of Hell, as it would have been constructed in
morality plays. It is unclear whether the actors playing Lucifer and Mephistopheles
appear, but Faustus does react to them. He shuns Lucifer, but there are various ways
in which an actor can interpret his response to Mephistopheles. The final denotative
stage direction, '*(The Devils) exeunt with him*', leaves the manner of their departure
up to the director.

The Chorus

In ancient Greece, the Chorus would consist of a group of masked singers who were
a vital part of the tragedy with several important functions. In the medieval morality
plays, there were sometimes single actors, separate from the drama, who performed
some of the functions of the Greek Chorus.

Functions

Marlowe uses the Chorus to offer important background and summary information.
The Prologue fills in the details of Faustus's lowly birth, his admission to Wittenberg
University, and his being awarded the title of Doctor of Divinity. In the Act 3 Chorus,
Wagner emphasises that Faustus seeks knowledge, not just the ability to play tricks.
Faustus has gone to Rome to 'prove' the knowledge he acquires for himself, not to
mock the Pope. In the Act 4 Chorus, we learn of Faustus's travels, the spectacular
improvement in his knowledge and his worldwide reputation. The Epilogue does not
need to add more information, only to remind us of what we have seen.

The speeches of the Chorus provide time for a scene change, create a sense of
time passing and remind the audience that they are watching a play. The Prologue
attracts the attention of the audience and prepares them to listen to the actors; the
Chorus ends his speech by pointing out Faustus in his study. In the Act 3 Chorus,
Wagner makes us feel that enough time has passed since Lucifer's visit for Faustus
to have learned a lot and be ready for 'some sport'. The Act 4 Chorus is needed to
tell us what happens during the 24 years that Faustus bargained for, since it involves
knowledge and acts which are literally 'out of this world' and cannot be demon-
strated on stage. This Chorus hints at Faustus's achievements, and tells us where the
next scene is set. The Epilogue brings the audience back to reality, reminding them
that this is a play, and mitigating the horror of the drama.

The Chorus also offers a sense of rich spectacle to the drama. In the Prologue,
the Chorus creates anticipation by reminding the audience of previous plays and

Marlowe's 'heavenly verse'. He uses impressive-sounding words like 'dalliance' and 'audacious' as well as classical references. He titillates the audience's appetite with talk of 'necromancy'. In the Act 3 Chorus, Wagner helps to give a flavour of what Faustus has gained through his pact: secret knowledge of astronomy, a chariot drawn by dragons to take him wherever he wishes to go. Once again, the Act 4 Chorus tells us what Faustus has gained — knowledge of 'the rarest things' and the hospitality of kings and emperors. In the Epilogue, the reference to 'Apollo's laurel bough' reminds us of Faustus's early promise, so makes his descent into Hell more tragic.

The Chorus offers commentary about and underlines the main themes of the play. The Prologue introduces the theme of excessive pride and ambition with references to Icarus and words from the semantic field of appetite. In the Act 3 Chorus, Wagner is impressed by Faustus's dedication to learning. The Act 4 Chorus is also impressed by Faustus's learning and his fame. In the Epilogue, the Chorus laments the fall of a 'learned man', underlining the tragic loss of a man who could have achieved 'Apollo's laurel bough', reminding us that, initially, Faustus had great potential.

The Chorus also tries to mould an audience's response to the unfolding drama. The Prologue expresses clear disapproval of Faustus's course of action with the words 'devilish' and 'cursed', and refers to Heaven as 'his chiefest bliss'. Wagner shows admiration for Faustus in the Act 3 Chorus and so does the Act 4 Chorus. The Epilogue instructs the audience how to respond, warning them 'only to wonder at unlawful things', not to practise them.

Language

It is interesting to explore how the language of each Chorus helps Marlowe to achieve his aims.

In the Prologue, the first person plural determiner in 'our Muse' (line 6) shows that the Chorus speaks on behalf of the company of actors. 'Muse' inflates the image of the playwright, saying that he is like the goddesses who inspired creative artists in Greek mythology. The Chorus talks of 'heavenly verse' (line 6), metaphorically suggesting that the poetry will be out of this world, like the music of the spheres, but also linking the poet with Christian morality, indicating from the start that he does not share Faustus's ambitions. In line 22, 'heavens' refers to the sun in the sky but also suggests God's disapproval. 'Swoll'n with cunning of a self-conceit' (line 20) introduces the extended metaphor of gorging on food until stuffed full. It also says that Faustus is puffed up with pride, and the phonological patterning of /s k s k/ allows the speaker to stress these words and sound disapproving. In lines 24 and 25, 'glutted' and 'surfeits', also from the semantic field of gorging on food, suggest excessive greed and similarly convey disapproval. 'Waxen wings' (line 21) links Faustus with Icarus who reached too high and fell into the sea.

In the Act 3 Chorus, Wagner makes classical references to 'Jove' and 'Olympus', and these help to suggest that Faustus has learned the secrets of the ancient gods. Marlowe cannot give details of what Faustus learns because it is beyond human knowledge. Neither can he perform impressive magic on stage, so we are invited to imagine it. Sixteenth-century playwrights also used 'Jove' as an alternative name for God, so Marlowe seems to be suggesting that Faustus blasphemously desires to know God's secrets, and that he is using the powers of Hell to try to find them out. Marlowe uses the magic of language to conjure up a fantastic image of Faustus travelling through the air in a burning chariot drawn by 'yoky dragons'. This demonstrates what Faustus has gained, which is difficult to show on a bare stage. Marlowe gives Wagner polysyllabic scientific terms such as 'astronomy' and 'cosmography' to impress the audience with Faustus's great learning. Faustus intends to 'prove cosmography', demonstrating that he is an empiricist; not content with being lectured by Mephistopheles, he intends to test his learning for himself.

In the Act 4 Chorus, the language suggests admiration: 'pleasure', 'rarest things', 'admired', 'wondered'. 'Things' is necessarily vague as we cannot know the secrets he learns. The tautology of 'royal' and 'of kings' makes the actor sound awed by the heights Faustus has reached, especially as he is now 'feasted' among the Emperor's nobles. The Chorus also tells us that Faustus does have friends, which is important because we only see Faustus with students, apart from Cornelius and Valdes at the beginning and an unnamed old man.

In the Epilogue, the sharply plosive monosyllable 'Cut' establishes a darkly violent tone for this final speech. The use of the passive voice means that Marlowe can retain the ambivalence regarding who or what has 'cut' the branch, who is responsible for Faustus's fall. The extended metaphor of the tree emphasises how unnatural Faustus's conduct has been and links neatly with the image of the laurel bough, which represents his early achievements in the fields of Divinity, Medicine and Analytics. The Chorus speaks directly to audience, commanding them to 'Regard' and take heed. He uses powerful adjectives, 'hellish' and 'fiendful', which, as well as literally recalling the action of the play, link Faustus with Hell and Lucifer, reminding the audience of Faustus's punishment. 'Fiendful fortune' is a clumsy piece of **alliteration**, as if Marlowe might be trying too hard to appease the censor. The tentative modal auxiliary 'may' suggests that 'the wise' may not take away the obvious lesson from the play. Marlowe has diplomatically distanced himself from his protagonist, but he seems to be questioning his own conclusion.

Form

Marlowe breaks the rhythm at times to achieve a particular effect. For instance, the Prologue opens with six lines of regular blank verse, establishing a measured and elevated tone, but, in line 7, Marlowe has reversed the iambic foot at the beginning, and this lays stress on the adverb, pointing the irony with wide-eyed

disingenuousness as everyone already knew that Faustus's fortunes were bad. The two mid-line caesuras round the ultra-polite 'gentlemen' slow the pace and point the irony still further. In line 20, the comma after the first syllable forces the speaker to pause and so lays extra emphasis on the derogatory adjective 'swoll'n'.

In line 25, there is no accent to suggest that 'cursed' is two syllables, so Marlowe seems to have weighted the disapproval by putting two heavily stressed syllables together, and the repetition of the velar plosive /k/ reinforces the tone. Once again, Marlowe reverses the iambic foot at the beginning of the next line to lay emphasis on the fact that, at this point, magic has surpassed everything else in Faustus's life, even his 'chiefest bliss' — his hope of an eternity in Heaven. In line 28, Marlowe ends the speech on a half-rhyme ('bliss'/'sits') as a signal that the Chorus has finished and the play is about to begin. It seems that the actor points to Faustus 'here', possibly drawing back the curtain to reveal Faustus in the inner stage under the minstrels' gallery.

In the first line of the Act 3 Chorus, the stress falls on the first syllable, and the short line allows the speaker to dwell on Faustus's great learning. Lines 3 and 5 also start with a stressed syllable encouraging the audience to feel awe at the information being imparted. It is worth noting that some words are intended to be slurred rather than spoken distinctly in order to keep the rhythm, e.g. 'in the' (line 3) and 'Being' (line 5). The caesuras round 'as I guess' draw attention to the fact that Wagner does not know what is going to happen, raising the audience's curiosity.

The internal rhyme in line 2 of the Act 4 Chorus, together with the alliteration of /r/ and /k/ create a **lyrical** tone to enhance the effect of the words. Line 12 opens with a stressed syllable to emphasise the information that Faustus has spent years acquiring so much knowledge that, by the time he returns to Wittenberg, the whole of the known world has heard of him. In consecutive lines, stress reversals also lay emphasis on the names of the Emperor and Faustus; the effect is to link the two names, as if they are of equal importance.

The first word of the Epilogue achieves extra impact through the stress reversal, and in line 4, a dramatic mid-line caesura invites a telling pause before the command. Another stress reversal in line 6 adds emphasis to 'Only', strengthening the message that the wise should not shun unlawful things altogether, but wonder at them. A rhyming couplet marks the end of the speech and the play.

Comedy

Contemporary accounts of performances of *Doctor Faustus* indicate that it was the comic appearances of devils that were the most popular parts of the play. Elizabethan theatres drew audiences from a wide cross-section of society, and they were used to watching morality plays in which comic buffoonery regularly alternated with scenes of high seriousness. In *Doctor Faustus* there are two sorts of comic scenes, those involving lower-class characters and those involving Faustus himself.

Lower-class characters

The theatre company would include some stand-up comedians who would take the parts of Wagner, Robin and Rafe. The actors would no doubt have improvised in order to gain more laughs, but in the text we can see that the play has been carefully structured. Simultaneously nonsensical and profound, the comic scenes clarify our perception of moral values. They force the audience to stand back and view Faustus objectively. To be properly appreciated, these comic scenes need to be studied in conjunction with the previous scene as each one parodies the previous scene, operating as a distorting mirror to expose the irony in the main plot.

In Act 1 scene 1, Faustus boasts about his academic achievements, but, in the following scene, Wagner outwits the Scholars with his insolent common sense. Faustus misuses terms we associate with God, such as 'heavenly' and 'divine'; Wagner takes God's name in vain, saying 'God in heaven knows' and he misuses religious **lexis**, 'my dear brethren', in his mockery. Faustus decides to try to 'gain a deity', but Wagner's joke about '*corpus naturale*' emphasises that Faustus is a man and not immortal. Faustus is anxious that he might die if he devotes his studies to magic, probably thinking of his soul, but, in the following scene, concern about his spiritual state is subverted into a question about his physical whereabouts. Wagner's cheeky reply, 'God in heaven knows' is more apt than he intends.

In Act 1 scene 3, Faustus tries to get a servant in Mephistopheles; in the following scene, Wagner tries to get Robin as a servant. Faustus tries to dictate the terms of his contract, and Robin tries to dictate terms, wanting the mutton well-roasted. Faustus has conjured Mephistopheles; Wagner conjures Balioll and Belcher, proving that you do not need great learning to conjure spirits. Faustus thinks he can control the spirit and use him to acquire great power; Robin thinks he can control devils, 'knock' and even kill them. Faustus agrees to sell his soul for 24 years of volup-tuousness. Robin wants to learn to conjure so that he can be intimate with women, disguised as a flea. Faustus arrogantly issues orders to Mephistopheles. Wagner is proud of having a servant and gives arrogant orders. However, whereas Faustus ignores the evidence to the contrary, Robin learns that he was deluded.

In Act 2 scene 1, Faustus demands a wife because he is 'wanton and lascivious'. In the following scene Robin and Rafe parody Faustus's sexual appetite with their obscene talk about what they will achieve now that Robin has stolen one of Faustus's conjuring books. In Act 3 scene 1, Faustus steals food and drink from the Pope, and his lofty ambitions are degraded by his trickery. In the following scene, Robin and Rafe steal a goblet from a vintner, and they are degraded by being transformed into animals. Their punishment for their presumption in conjuring Mephistopheles fore-shadows Faustus's punishment for his presumptuousness.

Comic scenes involving Faustus

In Act 2 scene 3, when Faustus feels remorse and begins to pray 'Ah Christ my Saviour,/ Seek to save distressèd Faustus' soul!', he is easily distracted from repentance by Lucifer and a show of the Seven Deadly Sins. The tone of the scene switches suddenly from tragedy to comedy. In the morality plays, Lucifer would have been as frightening as the company could make him so that they could pass round the hat before he would appear, and permanent theatres continued to make him a horrific figure. The sins are intended to be amusing, but they also invite us to laugh at Faustus's triviality and moral decay. The Young Vic production in 2002 made this more telling by having Faustus double as Pride and be expelled from a giant anus. In Act 2 scene 1, Faustus had declared 'The god thou servest is thine own appetite', and here his god of appetite is grotesquely parodied.

In Acts 3 and 4, Faustus and Mephistopheles appear to be comic double act, playing tricks on the Pope and his guest, the Knight at the Emperor's court and the Horse-courser. Putting horns on the Knight's head is the sort of bawdy joke the audience expects from Robin and Rafe, as horns were the conventional symbol of a cuckold — someone whose wife was unfaithful. These comic scenes demonstrate that Faustus's accomplishments grow increasingly petty as he wastes his limited time and his magical powers. However, although Faustus thinks he has gained control of Mephistopheles and the spirits, the audience is always aware of who is calling the tune and who is the deluded fool.

The scene with the Horse-courser mirrors Faustus's contract with Lucifer. Just as the Horse-courser thinks he is getting the best of the deal and learns too late that the 'horse' is worthless, so Faustus thinks he is gaining Mephistopheles as a servant and at his command, but realises too late that he is wrong. In the middle of the scene with the Horse-courser, he says in a soliloquy that 'Despair doth drive distrust unto my thoughts', so it seems that the farcical comedy emphasises Faustus's need to be distracted from his thoughts of despair. The comedy defuses the dramatic tension temporarily, and it enhances the tragedy through contrast.

Conclusion

For an audience of people who believed that devils were not only real but watching for opportunities to get human souls, the tension in the theatre must have been palpable at times. The comic scenes would have helped to release that tension for a few minutes before people's hearts once again rose into their mouths. However, for the majority of the audience, that delicious horror would have been even greater in the scenes involving lower-class characters, because these scenes demonstrate that Lucifer does not just target people with exceptional talent. Robin and Rafe were turned into animals for their presumption.

While laughing at the actors playing Faustus and Mephistopheles pretending to be invisible as they played tricks on the Pope and even gave him a box on the

ear, the audience would have been nervously wondering how many real invisible devils were among them. Indeed, as noted there are contemporary accounts of performances being abandoned in panic as extra devils were counted among the actors.

As more sceptical theatre-goers, we do not enjoy the scary element in the comic scenes, but we do appreciate the opportunity for a change of tone and pace from the relentless psychological drama being played out before us. Remove the comedy and the play becomes not more intense but less varied.

'Tragical History'

It seems that Marlowe intended the play to be a tragedy since the title page of the A-text calls the play a 'Tragical History'. Here are some of the definitions of 'tragedy' which were available to him:

(1) In the fourth century BC, Aristotle defined tragedy as: 'The imitation of an action that is serious and also, as having magnitude, complete in itself; in language with pleasurable accessories, each kind brought in separately in the parts of the work; in a dramatic, not in a **narrative** form; with incidents arousing pity and fear, wherewith to accomplish its catharsis of such emotions.' (*Poetics*)

It is not difficult to find 'pleasurable accessories' in the language, as in Aristotle's definition, nor points at which a production ought to arouse pity and fear. However, although the themes of *Doctor Faustus* are serious, not all of the action is. The play fits Aristotle's definition if we agree that the comic scenes actually enhance the tragedy, through reinforcement of themes and by raising awareness of how Faustus has wasted his talents.

(2) In the fourth century AD, Diomedes wrote that tragedy is a narrative about the fortunes of heroic or semi-divine characters.

If we define heroism as admirable courage or nobility, then it is difficult to argue that Faustus is a hero whom Diomedes would recognise. He is certainly not semi-divine, in spite of his aspirations.

(3) In the sixth and seventh centuries, Isidore of Seville observed that tragedy comprises sad stories about commonwealths and kings.

It is a sad story, but Isidore would not have considered Doctor Faustus a worthy protagonist for tragedy.

(4) In the twelfth century, John of Garland described tragedy as a poem written in the grand style about shameful and wicked deeds; a poem that begins in joy and ends in grief.

The play is predominantly written in poetry, some of which is in a grand style, as Garland requires, but can we really call Faustus's deeds 'shameful and wicked'? It could be argued that signing the contract is the only 'wicked' thing he actually does. The only film of the play emphasises Faustus's joy at the beginning by showing the ceremony and the celebrations when he was awarded his doctorate.

(5) In the fourteenth century, Chaucer wrote:

> Tragedie is to seyn a certeyn storie,
> As olde bookes maken us memorie,
> Of hym that stood in great prosperitee
> And is yfallen out of heigh degree
> Into miserie, and endeth wrecchedly. (*The Monk's Tale*)

Chaucer's definition fits *Doctor Faustus* better. At the beginning of the play, Faustus stands in high degree within the academic world, and he has the talents to become prosperous. Marlowe makes several references to his fall, and he ends wretchedly.

(6) A contemporary of Christopher Marlowe, Sir Philip Sidney, referred to:

> 'high and excellent Tragedy' that opens the greatest wounds and displays the ulcers covered with tissue; tragedy which makes kings fear to be tyrants and tyrants to 'manifest their tyrannical humours'. Tragedy stirs 'the affects of admiration and commiseration, teacheth the uncertainty of this world, and upon how weak foundations gilden roofs are builded'. (*Defence of Poesie*)

The Renaissance definition is interesting because the emphasis is more on the psychology of the individual. *Doctor Faustus* is the first play in the English language to open the mental wounds of its protagonist and display the ulcers of despair in the way we have come to expect in Shakespeare's tragedies.

Tragedy for the twenty-first century

Nowadays, people generally use the term 'tragedy' to refer to a merely sad or depressing story. However, even in literature it seems that the necessity for nobility has gone; tragedies are now written about ordinary people who have flaws and weaknesses that we recognise and possibly share. Modern tragic heroes bring about their own downfall, but there is often a tragic sense of inevitability about it. Until the last act, Faustus could have averted his fate; however, in a more secular age, the tragedy does not lie in what will happen after death but in the heroes' awareness that they have done something for which they cannot forgive themselves.

In *The Death of Tragedy* (1961), George Steiner argues that rationalism marks the death of tragedy, breaking man's sense of continuity with a divine realm. The triumph of rationalism and a secular worldview has removed the metaphysical grounds for tragedy in the modern world. The ancients saw themselves as a small but significant part of a much larger reality. Depicting life as a great mystery beyond human understanding, the great tragedies of the past 'instruct us how little of the

world belongs to man'. According to Steiner, modern man with his sciences and sceptical reason has conquered his superstitious belief in the unseen realm.

A tragic hero

According to Aristotle, a tragic hero is 'a man not pre-eminently virtuous and just, whose misfortune, however, is brought upon him not by vice and depravity but by some error of judgement, of the number of those in the enjoyment of great reputation and prosperity…The perfect plot, accordingly, must have a single, and not (as some tell us) a double issue; the change in the hero's fortunes must be not from misery to happiness, but on the contrary from happiness to misery; and the cause of it must not lie in any depravity, but in some great error on his part; the man himself being either such as we have described, or better, not worse, than that.'

The Greek term *hamartia*, translated above as an 'error of judgement', is ambiguous. It can either refer to an innate defect, commonly known as a tragic flaw, or a momentary lapse of judgement, which may arise from ignorance or some moral shortcoming. Faustus certainly enjoys great reputation and prosperity before the play opens. His misfortune is not brought upon him by vice and depravity, but by **hubris**, which we could call his tragic flaw especially since, when his pride has left him by the second Act, it has been replaced with despair, and this is the flipside of pride. He judges his own sins instead of humbly asking for God's forgiveness. However, it could be argued that he gambles that Hell is a fable, and this gamble turns out to be an error of judgement.

He begins to have doubts while he is waiting for Mephistopheles to return from Lucifer with approval of the contract. From this time on his resolve keeps faltering, and he fluctuates between an urge to repent and a terrible fear that, like Shakespeare's Macbeth, he is already 'in so far, that, should I wade no more,/ Returning were as tedious as go o'er' (III.iv.136–37). However, whereas Macbeth is a murderer who has sinned against his kinsman, his guest and his king, Faustus has not directly sinned against anyone. It seems that his error of judgement is in believing that, just by summoning Mephistopheles, he has put himself out of reach of God's mercy, and that a contract with Hell and the Devil is morally binding.

'Regard his hellish fall'

The concept of a fall from grace comes from the Bible. In the Bible we are told that 'there was war in heaven: Michael and his angels fought against the dragon; and the dragon fought against his angels,/ And prevailed not; neither was their place found any more in heaven./ And the great dragon was cast out, that old serpent, called the Devil, and Satan, which deceiveth the whole world: he was cast out into the earth, and his angels were cast out with him' (Revelations 12:7–9).

Mephistopheles tells Faustus that Lucifer was 'most dearly loved of God' and was thrown from the face of Heaven for 'aspiring pride and insolence'. Faustus also

aspires to 'gain a deity' and insolently asks 'What god can hurt thee, Faustus?' Mephistopheles is one of the 'unhappy spirits that fell with Lucifer'. The evicted angels physically fell from Heaven into Hell, which Mephistopheles describes as being 'within the bowels of these elements', just as Faustus probably falls physically through the trapdoor in the stage.

The angels fell morally from goodness to wickedness. Faustus went from excelling at the traditional fields of study to an attempt 'To practise more than heavenly power permits'. He has fallen from grace because he sought to climb above his allotted place in the Great Chain of Being. According to the A-text, Faustus fell because of his 'aspiring pride and insolence', but the B-text blames Mephistopheles who claims ''Twas I, that when thou wert i'the way to heaven,/ Dammed up thy passage'.

In the Prologue, Faustus is compared with Icarus, son of Daedalus, who made wings out of wax and feathers so that they could escape from Crete. Icarus was warned by his father not to fly too close to the sun, but, overwhelmed by the thrill of flying, he soared, the wax melted, and he fell into the sea. The story is a metaphor for the attempt to usurp the role of God and to attain divine knowledge. Like Icarus, Faustus disregarded the warnings and was carried away by his enthusiasm for divine knowledge, so, metaphorically, he was 'falling to a devilish exercise'. Icarus's fall marked the end of his life, but Faustus's fall marks a beginning. To 'fall to' means to begin something, usually a meal, so the eating metaphors of 'glut' and 'surfeit' are particularly appropriate. However, we are told that the 'heavens conspired his overthrow', so there is a suggestion that Faustus did not fall but was thrown out.

Faustus begins to fall when he seeks 'profit', 'delight', 'power', 'honour', 'omnipotence' and decides to try his brains to 'gain a deity'. Marlowe uses the word when one of the scholars fears that 'he is fallen into that damned art' for which Cornelius and Valdes are infamous.

Gothic elements

Mary Shelley wrote in the introduction to her **Gothic** novel, *Frankenstein*, that her intention was to write a story 'which would speak to the mysterious fears of our nature, and awaken thrilling horror — one to make the reader dread to look round, to curdle the blood and quicken the beatings of the heart'.

Writers have always exploited the way in which readers or theatre-goers enjoy the thrill of being scared. *Beowulf* would probably not have delighted listeners and readers for more than a millennium, if the composer had not introduced terrifying monsters to threaten the harmony of the mead-hall. The word 'Gothic', however, was not used as a literary term until 1764 when Horace Walpole wrote *The Castle of Otranto: A Gothic Story*. In using the word 'Gothic', he was evoking an ancient Germanic tribe from the so-called 'Dark Ages' that lost its ethnic identity in the sixth century. Originally the term simply implied 'medieval', but it has now become a term that embraces elements of violence, death, horror, the supernatural and the macabre. Gothic fiction, in whatever medium, works by introducing the unfamiliar, the inexplicable and the irrational into a familiar, safe and realistic world. They are tales of mystery and fear, designed to chill the spine, but only enough to evoke a delightful horror.

Although Marlowe did not set out to write a Gothic story, there are several elements that we now recognise as Gothic in *Doctor Faustus*. The Prologue awakens thrilling horror when he tells how Faustus fell 'to a devilish exercise' and 'surfeits upon cursed necromancy'. This would have been enhanced with a real fear by Marlowe's original audience who believed in devils and would have dreaded to look round in case Faustus had actually conjured one. As we know, there is documentary evidence that sometimes people believed there were extra devils on stage, and, at least once, the theatre was emptied as a result.

Monstrous apparitions are another common feature of Gothic literature. When Mephistopheles first appears, he looks 'too ugly' and frightening. Marlowe's source describes a creature of fire. The B-text says that Mephistopheles enters in the shape of a dragon. On the title page of the 1624 and 1631 editions, the woodcut shows a grotesque creature that could possibly be rising up out of the trapdoor in the stage. Lucifer and Beelzebub also appear looking 'terrible', and when minor devils appear, their horror is often enhanced with fireworks. The Sins would probably be monstrous apparitions as well, but Marlowe leaves their appearance up to the director's imagination, and they would probably have been comic monstrosities.

Another Gothic element is the manifestation of demonic powers. We are treated to the pageant of the Seven Deadly Sins, and told about Faustus's travels in a fiery chariot drawn by dragons. Mephistopheles makes horns grow on the knight's head, and he conjures up apparitions of Alexander the Great and his paramour, as well as Helen of Troy. Not only do we see numerous devils, but we also watch the effects of demonic intervention when the Old Man is 'menaced' (5.1.113–18) and Faustus is physically prevented from repenting (5.2.27–30; 5.2.69).

Marlowe sets the beginning of his play quite realistically in the study of a university don; however, productions often introduce Gothic elements such as skulls or skeletons. The doom-laden atmosphere is continued when the Good Angel warns of God's wrath. In the next scene, the Scholars reinforce this with their fear that nothing can reclaim Faustus. Marlowe invokes a sinister setting, appropriately 'gloomy', 'drizzling' and 'pitchy', in the first four lines of 1.3 when Faustus is about to conjure a devil. Like Faustus, Mary Shelley's Victor Frankenstein resorts to demonic powers when he calls on 'you, spirits of the dead; and you, wandering ministers of vengeance, to aid and conduct me in my work'. He, too, 'carried about with me my eternal hell'.

Psychological terror

Marlowe's hero is in the direst of imaginable straits, but he refuses to listen to others. Mephistopheles's warnings, and especially his epistrophe (1.3.71–73), do not affect Faustus, but they lead the audience to expect the worst. The atmosphere of doom and gloom does not hit Faustus until Act 2 when he begins to fear that he has gone too far to be saved. Marlowe introduces another scary supernatural element when Faustus reads '*homo fuge*' on his arm, possibly warning him to flee from the wrath of God. At the end of 1.1, Faustus thinks he may be in danger of dying, but he is risking far more than his life; he is risking his chance of salvation. This would have spoken forcefully to the mysterious fears of Marlowe's original audience.

Even if we do not fear supernatural intervention, Marlowe presents us with tense psychological terror throughout the play, and this reaches its climax as Faustus finally realises that he has lost his gamble and has 'but one bare hour to live'. His fear is graphically conveyed as he tries everything he can think of to escape an eternity in Hell. He learns the uselessness of his magic as he attempts to command the elements. He tries vainly to repent, saying 'O I'll leap up to my God! Who pulls me down?' At the end of the hour, '*Thunder and lightning*' accompany Faustus's final moments on earth. Faustus declares 'Ugly hell, gape not', so Marlowe seems to be expecting a literal 'mouth of Hell', as there had been in the morality plays, to be revealed on stage. However, it is not the devils that accompany him to the mouth of Hell which terrify a modern audience, but the psychological horror as he begs for the total annihilation of his soul.

Audience reactions

Marlowe has constructed the play so that, through the Choruses and the Angels, we are expected to look at Faustus objectively and pass judgement on his behaviour. However, Faustus's soliloquies invite us to understand him from the inside, and we also respond subjectively to what he says and does. This means that sometimes we are led to sympathise with him, and at other times we become frustrated with his foolishness.

Prologue

Although we are apparently expected to condemn Faustus for his pride, the audience might admire him for his ambition and his great scholarship. There is even a suggestion that he is a tragic victim of supernatural forces who 'conspired his overthrow'.

Act 1

The audience might sympathise with Faustus's disaffection with conventional branches of learning and applaud his desire to make his mark upon the world. However, he is arrogant in the way he boasts about his academic successes, and he employs false logic to convince himself that he is doing the right thing. Nevertheless, he makes magic sound so exciting that perhaps the audience is also enticed by the possibilities. He has studied the Scriptures and been made a Doctor of Divinity, so the Good Angel is not offering anything new. By contrast, the Evil Angel offers fresh knowledge and power.

It is not so much what he and his friends say that encourages us to sympathise with his ambitions, but Marlowe's poetry. The rhythms of the rhetoric encourage **empathy** rather than criticism. The audience may admire Faustus for his courage in being prepared to die in the pursuit of knowledge and power, instead of condemning him for his blasphemous behaviour. Admiration for his courage and erudition may soon turn to condemnation of his arrogance and his foolishness in refusing to listen to Mephistopheles. It is frustrating that such an intelligent man can be so blind to the obvious!

Act 2 scene 1

While Faustus waits for Mephistopheles to return from Lucifer, he is in a different mood. He has realised his mistake, but he thinks he has already gone too far. Marlowe invites our sympathy for him, as it is a familiar human failing to regret past actions and believe it is too late to try to put them right. An audience might be reminded of how Claudius manipulates Laertes into proving his love for his father, Polonius, who was killed by Hamlet, by recklessly offering 'To cut his throat i'th'church'. Faustus makes a similar extravagant gesture, which nobody could condone, offering 'lukewarm blood of new-born babes'. The Angels invite us to consider Faustus objectively, and then his response to them is so arrogant and misguided that it is difficult to feel sympathy.

Faustus is a gambler; he has already 'hazarded' his soul. How much sympathy do we have for a gambler who ignores advice, ignores the warning of his own body when his blood congeals, and twice ignores a supernatural warning on his arm? Do we sympathise with his determination or are we frustrated that he is so obstinate? How can he be so foolish as to be persuaded by a show of devils? The audience knows the story, but Marlowe wants us to continue to hope that he will repent.

Act 2 scene 3

Mephistopheles miscalculates and contradicts what he said earlier about Heaven. Faustus picks this up and starts to repent, so once again the audience hopes he will. The Good Angel reminds us that Faustus could still repent, has done nothing irreversible yet, but we become exasperated because he listens to the Evil Angel.

Faustus sees his choice as continuing on his course to damnation or committing suicide. Marlowe invites us to sympathise with the agonies of his despair. Gradually he realises that he has sold his soul for knowledge that he already has, but is he fair to blame Mephistopheles?

Once again we are reminded that Faustus still has a choice and this time he goes further than before on the road to repentance, calling on Christ to save his soul. Once again our hopes and sympathies are evoked. He seems really terrified by the appearance of Lucifer and Beelzebub, thinking that they have come to take his soul already. Perhaps it is relief that makes him susceptible to the pageant of the sins, but it is difficult to sympathise with his gullibility.

Act 3

Empathy with his delight in glamorous foreign travel soon gives way to contempt for the way he wastes his gifts on playing silly tricks. The audience might also give a shiver of fear at the humiliation of God's representative and the realisation that the Pope is powerless against the forces of evil.

Act 4

The audience might feel frustration that Faustus is so humble with the Emperor, when at first he aspired to be greater than an emperor, and that he is merely a conjuror and grateful for patronage. However, we might sympathise with him in his fatalistic awareness that the time is approaching when he must pay his debt. The audience is even more frustrated that he wastes his talent playing tricks on a dishonest horse-dealer. However, his brief soliloquy invites sympathy with his despair, especially when we learn that he has not slept for eight nights, but then, instead of taking action, he consoles himself with the foolish hope that he will have time to repent in the future. We may be even more irritated by his humility and the way he wastes his talent as he entertains the duke and duchess.

Act 5 scene 1

Perhaps if we could see Faustus at his last meal, we could be made to sympathise with him, but Marlowe distances us from him, and we wonder why he is behaving frivolously when his end is so close.

Faustus is kind to the Scholars, warning them of the danger of speaking to Helen, clearly wanting to protect them rather than take them with him to Hell. The Old Man is unfairly vindictive in his accusations — Faustus has committed no 'heinous sins' — so the audience can sympathise with Faustus and even admire his sense of honour in not wanting to break his promise to Lucifer. However, we know that this is misguided, so we are still rooting for him, hoping that he will repent. It begins to look as if he will, then he sends the Old Man away and is vulnerable to Mephistopheles' threats. Once again we are invited to find it frustrating that Faustus gives in to the weak threat of 'I'll in piecemeal tear thy flesh' (especially when we see the Old Man happily going up to Heaven while the devils do their worst). Marlowe once again invites us to empathise with the agonies of Faustus's despair, but only until he spitefully asks Mephistopheles to torment the Old Man.

Faustus does not turn to God when Mephistopheles admits that he can do little because the Old Man's faith is strong. He seems to foolishly think that, in order to be true to himself, he must honour his contract. Then he knowingly commits the sin of demoniality and puts himself beyond redemption. He seems to delude himself that the succubus disguised as Helen, who has sucked forth his soul, can give him his soul again.

Act 5 scene 2

Surely the audience should be expected to sympathise with Faustus as we watch the actor try in vain to weep, to pray, to lift his hands to Heaven, and then warn the Scholars to leave him. As he delivers the final soliloquy, the actor tries in vain to leap up to God; then he excitedly sees a vision of Christ's blood and is apparently tortured in front of our eyes. Terrified, he grovels away from a vision of angry God, trying in vain to find a hiding place. Even if we do not sympathise with him because he brought it upon himself, it is impossible to be objective as we watch the actor and listen to his terrified tone of voice as he is dragged down to Hell.

Epilogue

The audience is expected to regret the waste of potential and to learn by Faustus's example, but we are still encouraged to 'wonder at unlawful things'.

Significant differences in the B-text

Act 1 scene 3

In the B-text the stage direction reads: '*Thunder. Enter Lucifer and four Devils (above). (Enter) Faustus to them with this speech. (He holds a book, unaware of their presence)*'. The presence of Lucifer and the devils removes some of the suspense, as we know that Faustus will be successful, but none of the fear. He is a pawn in a cosmic game played out by the powers of Heaven and Hell.

Act 3 scene 1

In the B-text Faustus and Mephistopheles rescue the rival German Pope, Bruno, from Pope Adrian at the Vatican by sending the cardinals to sleep and impersonating

them. There is also more evidence of the amazing experiences Faustus gained from his contract:

> FAUSTUS   Thou know'st within the compass of eight days
> (*to Meph.*):   We viewed the face of heaven, of earth, and hell.
> So high our dragons soared into the air
> That, looking down, the earth appeared to me
> No bigger than my hand in quantity.
> There did we view the kingdoms of the world,
> And what might please mine eye I there beheld. (lines 68–74)

In the A-text, the Pope is a comic caricature, but in the B-text he is shown to be arrogant, vindictive and vengeful. The B-text comes out much more strongly against Roman Catholicism, and Faustus actually achieves a heroic rescue rather than being portrayed as a mere trickster:

> POPE ADRIAN   To me and Peter shalt thou grovelling lie
> (*to Bruno*):   And crouch before the papal dignity.
> Sound trumpets, then, for thus Saint Peter's heir
> From Bruno's back ascends Saint Peter's chair.
> *A flourish while he ascends*
> Thus, as the gods creep on with feet of wool
> So shall our sleeping vengeance now arise
> And smite with death thy hated enterprise. (lines 94–101)

The Pope proudly believes that he has unlimited power and can do whatever he likes, which is what Faustus desires. The powers of Hell defeat him in this instance, however, and the Pope is revealed to be another overreacher who does not have the power he thought he had:

> POPE ADRIAN: Is not all power on earth bestowed on us?
> And therefore, though we would, we cannot err.
> Behold this silver belt, whereto is fixed
> Seven golden keys fast sealed with seven seals
> In token of our sevenfold power from heaven,
> To bind or loose, lock fast, condemn, or judge,
> Resign, or seal, or whatso pleaseth us. (lines 151–57)

Act 3 scene 2

In the B-text, Bruno is sent flying back to Germany, and the Pope learns of Bruno's escape. The B-text directly confronts the split between Protestant and Catholic when the German Emperor and Bruno are condemned because they are Protestant heretics:

> POPE ADRIAN   Did I not tell you
> (*to the cardinals*):   Tomorrow we would sit i'th'consistory
> And there determine of his punishment?
> You brought us word even now, it was decreed

> That Bruno and the cursèd emperor
> Were by the holy council both condemned
> For loathèd Lollards and base schismatics. (lines 36–42)

The Pope is angry and vindictive, even to his own cardinals. This scene suddenly stops being comic as the innocent are taken away to be tortured, leaving the audience thinking that Faustus might be right to fear the wrath of God.

> POPE ADRIAN By Peter, you shall die
> (*to the cardinals*): Unless you bring them forth immediately. —
> Hale them to prison. Lade their limbs with gyves! —
> False prelates, for this hateful treachery
> Curst be your souls to hellish misery. (lines 50–54)

Act 4 scene 1

The German Emperor is grateful to Faustus for freeing Bruno, praising and honouring him, before asking to see Alexander. This vision is extended in the B-text, so that the Emperor gets carried away and goes to embrace the figures. Faustus's reaction suggests that he knows that there is danger in embracing spirits, so, when he embraces Helen, he knows what he is risking:

> (*Enter Mephistopheles. A*) *Sennet. Enter at one (door) the Emperor Alexander, at the other Darius. They meet; Darius is thrown down. Alexander kills him, takes off his crown, and, offering to go out, his Paramour meets him. He embraceth her and sets Darius' crown upon her head; and coming back, both salute the (German) Emperor, who, leaving his state, offers to embrace them, which Faustus seeing suddenly stays him. Then trumpets cease and music sounds*
> FAUSTUS: My gracious lord, you do forget yourself.
>   These are but shadows, not substantial. (lines 102–03)

Act 4 scene 2

In the B-text, the Knight has a name, Benvolio, which means 'well-wisher' and suggests that he is one of the good characters, able to recognise diabolic powers, but he is not able to defeat them. He plots Faustus's death with friends. When Faustus enters, wearing a false head, Benvolio strikes off the false head, and Faustus rises and says:

> FAUSTUS   Knew you not, traitors, I was limited
> (*to the*   For four-and-twenty years to breathe on earth?
> *conspirators*): And had you cut my body with your swords,
>   Or hewed this flesh and bones as small as sand,
>   Yet in a minute had my spirit returned,
>   And I had breathed a man made free from harm.
>   But wherefore do I dally my revenge?
>   Ashtaroth, Belimoth, Mephistopheles!
>   *Enter Mephistopheles and other Devils (Belimoth and Ashtaroth)*
>   Go horse these traitors on your fiery backs,

And mount aloft with them as high as heaven;
Thence pitch them headlong to the lowest hell.
Yet stay. The world shall see their misery,
And hell shall after plague their treachery. (lines 71–83)

Like the Pope, Faustus thinks he is inviolate. This reminds the audience that, in the contract, the first condition he made was that 'Faustus may be a spirit in form and substance', and it foreshadows the final scene of the B-text in which the Scholars find his dismembered body.

Act 5 scene 1

In the B-text the Old Man, unlike the hell-fire preacher of the A-text, is unfailingly kind and compassionate, even apologising for his speech in case it sounds like a lecture. Here is a true friend, a man not an angel, reminding Faustus that he can still repent, and that he is not a spirit yet. This makes it even more surprising that Faustus should turn on the Old Man so spitefully, and more tragic that Faustus feels bound to his contract, even though it is not as binding as he believes:

OLD MAN: It may be this my exhortation
Seems harsh and all unpleasant. Let it not,
For, gentle son, I speak it not in wrath
Or envy of thee, but in tender love
And pity of thy future misery;
And so have hope that this my kind rebuke,
Checking thy body, may amend thy soul. (lines 44–50)

Unlike in the A-text, the Old Man does not reappear when Faustus is with Helen.

Act 5 scene 2

In the A-text, Faustus's tragedy is a private one; he is alone with his conscience, his fear, his remorse. In the B-text, Lucifer, Beelzebub and Mephistopheles enter above, presumably in the minstrels' gallery, to watch Faustus during his last hour on earth. The presence of the powers of Hell above emphasises the tragedy of his position as he struggles to assert his own individuality, and it might be interpreted as taking away Faustus's free will and reducing him to a puppet. Similarly, in *Macbeth*, the appearance of Hecate, 'the close contriver of all harms', suggests that he is being controlled by evil powers.

Mephistopheles understands Faustus well and he chillingly predicts Faustus's final descent into despair. However, the suspense is lessened by the sight of the devils hovering to take his soul to Hell at the end of the 24 years.

BEELZEBUB: And here we'll stay
To mark him how he doth demean himself.
MEPHISTOPHELES: How should he, but in desperate lunacy?
Fond worldling, now his heart-blood dries with grief;
His conscience kills it, and his labouring brain

> Begets a world of idle fantasies
> To overreach the devil. But all in vain.
> His store of pleasures must be sauced with pain. (lines 9–16)

The B-text offers a more conventional morality pattern for a Jacobean audience, in which the tempter has been at work since the beginning. It is not until the final act that the audience learns that Mephistopheles distracted Faustus from his studies of theology even before the play opened. Mephistopheles claims to have prevented him from knowledge of the Atonement, whereby Christ's death expiates all our sins and makes salvation possible to those who truly repent. Faustus's rejection of divinity in the opening scene is made through incomplete knowledge of the Gospels, not a wilful rejection of God's promise to justify turning to necromancy:

MEPHISTOPHELES:	Ay, Faustus, now thou hast no hope of heaven;
	Therefore despair. Think only upon hell,
	For that must be thy mansion, there to dwell.
FAUSTUS:	O thou bewitching fiend, 'twas thy temptation
	Hath robbed me of eternal happiness.
MEPHISTOPHELES:	I do confess it, Faustus, and rejoice.
	'Twas I that, when thou wert i'the way to heaven,
	Dammed up thy passage. When thou took'st the book
	To view the Scriptures, then I turned the leaves
	And led thine eye.
	What, weep'st thou? 'Tis too late. Despair, farewell!
	Fools that will laugh on earth must weep in hell.
	(lines 86–97)

If we take this addition into account, it means that Mephistopheles' apparent friendship was a kind of double bluff; he was arrogantly testing Faustus to see how foolish, how presumptuous he was, knowing that Faustus would not listen to his warnings. Any sympathy we might have felt for Mephistopheles is dispelled as we realise that he was putting on an act.

In the B-text, the Good and Bad Angels are no longer in conflict; now they speak in unison, even sharing lines and rhymes. While music plays, representing harmony, the throne is lowered onto the stage, reminding the audience that, in seeking power, Faustus has actually forfeited the kingdom of heaven:

GOOD ANGEL:	O Faustus, if thou hadst given ear to me,
	Innumerable joys had followed thee.
	But thou didst love the world.
BAD ANGEL:	Gave ear to me,
	And now must taste hell's pains perpetually.
GOOD ANGEL:	O, what will all thy riches, pleasures, pomps
	Avail thee now?
BAD ANGEL:	Nothing but vex thee more,
	To want in hell, that had on earth such store.
	Music while the throne descends

| GOOD ANGEL: | O, thou hast lost celestial happiness, |
| | Pleasures unspeakable, bliss without end. (lines 97–106) |

In the B-text, '*Hell is discovered*', possibly by drawing the curtain at the back of the stage and revealing a painted backcloth with graphic pictures of torture. The Bad Angel describes the horrors and hints at tortures even more horrid, suggesting that the imagination causes more pain than any physical torture can. Hell is both a state of mind, as Mephistopheles told Faustus in 1.3, and a place:

	(The throne ascends.) Exit (Good Angel). Hell is discovered
BAD ANGEL:	Now, Faustus, let thine eyes with horror stare
	Into that vast perpetual torture-house.
	There are the Furies tossing damnèd souls
	On burning forks; their bodies boil in lead.
	There are live quarters broiling on the coals,
	That ne'er can die. This ever-burning chair
	Is for o'er-tortured souls to rest them in.
	These that are fed with sops of flaming fire
	Were gluttons, and loved only delicates,
	And laughed to see the poor starve at their gates.
	But yet all these are nothing. Thou shalt see
	Ten thousand tortures that more horrid be. (lines 115–26)

Faustus's long soliloquy comes after the Bad Angel leaves as the clock strikes eleven, but the devils are still watching.

Act 5 scene 3

In the B-text, the Scholars find Faustus's dismembered body and take it for burial. This short scene provides an anti-climax after Faustus's intensely powerful final soliloquy. It possibly reinforces God's mercy in that even Faustus will be given 'due burial', a service in which prayers will be said for his soul, but the irony is that these prayers are now irrelevant; it is too late.

Conclusion

It is likely that neither text represents the play as it was originally written by Marlowe in approximately 1588. The A-text was not printed until 11 years after his death. The B-text, printed 12 years later than the A-text, has additional scenes which present Faustus as an anti-Catholic hero and Mephistopheles as a more traditional tempter. The B-text also has more stage business and farcical comedy and this detracts from the play's subtle psychological portrait of Faustus, so that, whereas the A-text emerges as a personal tragedy, the B-text becomes a morality play with an unhappy ending.

Glossary

Achilles: the most handsome of the heroes assembled against Troy in the Trojan War in Greek mythology When he was born, his mother, the nymph Thetis, holding him by his heel, immersed him in the River Styx in an attempt to make him immortal, so Achilles was invulnerable in all of his body except for his heel. He was killed by an arrow shot in the heel by Paris.

Actaeon: a hunter who came across the goddess **Diana** (Artemis) while she was bathing in the woods. As a punishment for watching her, he was turned into a stag and torn to pieces by his own hounds. He is significant as a parallel to Faustus because he lusted after something forbidden and was destroyed by it. In the B-text, Faustus is 'torn asunder' at the end, like Actaeon, suggesting the traditional punishment for pride, which was to be broken on the wheel.

Agrippa, Cornelius (1486–1535): a German magician, writer of occult books, theologian, astrologer and alchemist, who apparently rejected magic two years before his death. Nevertheless, after his death rumours circulated that he had summoned demons.

Alexander (2.3.27): another name for Paris, a Trojan prince, son of King Priam and Hecuba. He was in love with the nymph Oenone, but he was chosen by Zeus to judge which of three goddesses was the fairest. Aphrodite bribed him to choose her, promising him the love of the most beautiful woman in the world. He ignored everyone's advice and went to Sparta to abduct his reward, Helen, wife of Menelaus. After he was wounded in the Trojan War, he asked to be carried to Oenone, but, angry at his desertion, she refused to help him. After his death she hanged herself from grief.

Alexander the Great (356–323 BC): one of the most successful military commanders of all time. By the time he died, he had conquered nearly all the world known to the ancient Greeks.

Apollo: the Greek and Roman god of prophecy and divination, the god of healing, the patron of music and the arts, and the leader of the **Muses**.

Arethusa: a nymph with whom the river god Alpheus fell in love when she bathed in his waters. She fled from his embrace to the island of Ortygia at the entrance to the bay of Syracuse in Sicily, where she was turned by Artemis into a spring. Alpheus did not give up his love but flowed beneath the sea to Ortygia and mingled his waters with hers.

Aristotle (384–322 BC): a Greek scholar who became one of the most important founding figures in Western philosophy. *Poetics* is the title given to two of Aristotle's works on the nature of proof in argument.

Bacon, Roger (c. 1219–94): (also known as *Doctor Mirabilis*: 'wonderful teacher') was an Oxford philosopher and Franciscan friar who placed considerable emphasis on empiricism, championing experimental study over reliance on authority. He is

credited with being the first experimental scientist. He was also an eminent astrologer and alchemist.

Constantinople: a Greek city that fell to the Turks in 1453. In the sixteenth century, it was the largest and richest city in Europe, the capital of the Ottoman Empire. It was renamed Istanbul in 1930.

D'Abano, Pietro (c. 1250–1316): an Italian philosopher, astrologer and professor of medicine at the University of Padua. He was tried as a heretic because he endeavoured to account for the wonderful effects in nature by the influence of the celestial bodies rather than accepting orthodox doctrine that attributed them to angels or demons. He died before the trial ended.

Dardania: one of the names given to Troy.

Dee, Dr John (1527–1608/9): a devout polymath who believed it was his sacred duty to harness the occult forces of the universe for the benefit of mankind. He wrote a number of influential books, including ones on mathematics, geometry, navigation, geography, astronomy, philosophy and chemistry. Like Marlowe, he was a member of Raleigh's School of Night. He was court astrologer to Elizabeth, who used to visit him at his home in Mortlake where he had the largest library in England.

Diana: a goddess (Diana to the Romans, Artemis to the Greeks), who was believed to roam the mountains and forests with her attendant nymphs, delighting in the hunt and who had taken a vow of chastity. When Actaeon watched her bathing naked with her nymphs, she grew angry, splashed him with water and transformed his body into a stag, although his mind remained the same, so he realised the full horror of his fate when his hounds tore him apart.

Elements: earth, air, fire, water — of which it was believed in the Middle Ages that the universe was composed, with corresponding humours to explain human temperament.

Gorboduc (1561): the first English tragedy, it was written in blank verse and full of high-sounding moral sayings known as *sententiae*. It was written for the law students of the Inner Temple, not for public performance.

Helen of Troy: the daughter of Zeus and Leda, she was married to Menelaus, King of Sparta. Some years later, Paris, a Trojan prince, came and abducted Helen. She was restored to Menelaus after the Trojan War was launched to reclaim her. The myth confirms the medieval theological belief that men's downfall is ultimately caused by women.

Homer (eighth century BC): a legendary ancient Greek epic poet who composed the *Iliad* and the *Odyssey*. Homer is traditionally held to be blind.

Humanists: they were originally people who studied the humanities and, through studying classical literature, developed a philosophy, humanism, which contradicted the traditional medieval view of what it meant to be human. Instead of regarding man as 'fallen' and full of sin, humanists affirm the dignity and worth of people and encourage individual aspiration.

Humours: four bodily fluids thought to be produced by different organs and related to one of the four elements, an excess of which was said to cause particular temperaments: yellow bile (anger), blood (happiness), phlegm (calm), black bile (melancholy).

Icarus: the son of Daedalus. According to Greek mythology, Daedalus, a brilliant inventor, was exiled from Athens after murdering his nephew and he sought refuge in Crete. He built the Labyrinth in which the Minotaur was kept, and he provided Theseus with the ball of thread which enabled him to kill the Minotaur. As punishment, King Minos imprisoned Daedalus and Icarus in the Labyrinth, and Daedalus made wings so that he and his son, Icarus, could escape. Icarus ignored his father's warning and flew too near the sun. The wax holding the feathers in place melted, and he fell into the sea. The fall of Icarus became a popular Renaissance emblem of the 'heroic overreacher', illustrating the danger of soaring aspiration. The reference acts as another parallel to Faustus who ignores God's warnings, reaches to forbidden heights and falls.

Machiavelli, Niccolò (1469–1527): an Italian philosopher, writer and politician. He was the first to assert the view that religion is designed to keep men in awe. 'Machiavellian' has become a derogatory term because, in *The Prince*, he argued that the greatest moral good is a virtuous and stable state, and actions to protect the country are therefore justified even if they are cruel. This has been interpreted as a philosophy of ruthless pragmatism and self-interest.

Menelaus: see **Helen of Troy**

Oenone: see **Alexander**

Olympus: the highest mountain in Greece and home of the gods of Greek mythology.

Paris: see **Alexander**

Penelope: the wife of Ulysses (Odysseus) and the heroine of Homer's epic poem, the *Odyssey*. She remained faithful to her husband during his 20-year absence at the Trojan War.

Puritanism: originally a pejorative term used to describe the beliefs of those who felt that the Elizabethan Religious Settlement of 1559 had not gone far enough to remove Roman Catholic elements from the Church of England. Puritans believed in the individual acting according to the dictates of his/her conscience, rather than in accordance with instructions from the established Church.

Pythagoras: a Greek mathematician, scientist and philosopher who lived in the sixth century BC.

Saba: an alternative spelling of 'Sheba'. There is some debate about the kingdom of Sheba. It may have been where Yemen is, or Ethiopia, or both. The Queen of Sheba tested Solomon 'with hard questions' (1 Kings 10: 1).

The School of Night: because England had broken from the Catholic Church and European monarchs schemed to replace Elizabeth, the Queen and her council were

in constant fear of too much freedom of thought and expression, thinking that radical new ideas might destabilise the monarchy. When Sir Walter Raleigh and Lord Henry Percy gathered together a group of people who dared to discuss new and inventive ideas that might give England an edge over her enemies, they kept their activities secret. This secret group consisted of forward-thinking intellectuals, courtiers and educated commoners, including mathematicians, astronomers, voyagers, philosophers and poets.

Semele: in Greek mythology, Zeus fell in love with Semele and repeatedly visited her secretly. Foolishly, Semele asked Zeus to reveal himself in all his glory, instead of disguising himself as a mortal. Humans cannot survive after looking on the glory of the king of the gods, and she perished, consumed in lightning-ignited flame.

Seneca (first century AD): a Roman writer whose tragic plays were written for reading and recitation rather than performance. They are highly rhetorical in style and the dialogue is more like debate than conversation. There is usually a heavy atmosphere of doom and inevitability over the whole play. His plays were the model for *Gorboduc*.

Wittenberg: in 1502, a Protestant university was founded at Wittenberg in Germany. Noted for scepticism and free intellectual enquiry, Wittenberg is closely associated with Martin Luther, who, in 1517, nailed his 95 theses against the selling of indulgences at the church door. This marks the beginning of the Protestant Reformation. It is no accident that both Faustus and Hamlet attend the University of Wittenberg, because both characters are seen to question orthodox opinions.

Literary terms and concepts

The terms and concepts below have been selected for their relevance to talking and writing about *Doctor Faustus*. It will aid argument and expression to become familiar with them and to use them in your discussion and essays, provided that you can support them with examples from the text and explain their effect.

allegory	a story that can be interpreted on two levels: as a surface narrative and at a deeper level that is often didactic and moralistic. Characters and episodes are intended to represent some elements in human life. The Good and Evil Angels as well as the Seven Deadly Sins are allegorical figures
alliteration	repetition of initial sound in adjacent words to create an atmospheric or onomatopoeic effect, e.g. 'pretty…paltry' (1.1.30)
ambiguity	capacity of words to have two simultaneous meanings in the context as a device for enriching meaning, e.g. 'heavenly'
ambivalence	the co-existence in one person's mind of two opposing attitudes or feelings in a single context

antithesis	a contrast or opposition of ideas, usually by the balancing of connected clauses with parallel grammatical constructions
archaic	of language: **diction** or grammar no longer in current use at the time of writing, e.g. 'anon' for 'now'
bawdy	creating humour through references to sex which are in bad taste
blank verse	unrhymed **iambic pentameter**, the staple form in Marlowe's and Shakespeare's plays
caesura	deliberate break or pause in a line of poetry, signified by punctuation
catharsis	the Greek word for 'purgation'. Aristotle used 'catharsis' to describe the way tragedy, having aroused powerful feelings in the spectator, also has a therapeutic effect; after the storm and climax there comes a sense of release from tension, of calm
characterisation	means by which fictional characters are personified and made distinctive
climax	moment of intensity to which a series of events has been leading
connotations	associations evoked by a word, e.g. 'glutted', 'surfeits'
contextuality	historical, social and cultural background of a text
convention	a practice established by usage or agreement, e.g. the invisibility robe Faustus wears in 3.1
corruptio optimi pessima est	a Latin tag meaning 'the corruption of the best becomes the worst'. Because Lucifer was the brightest of the angels, he is now the worst of the devils
criticism	evaluation of literary text or other artistic work
diction	choice of words; vocabulary from a particular **semantic field**
double entendre	expression with two meanings, one of them coarse, e.g. 'horns', 'clefts' (1.4.53–54)
dramatic irony	when the audience knows something the character speaking does not, which creates humour or tension, e.g. beginning of 5.2
elision	omission of sound(s) and letter(s) for metrical regularity in verse, e.g. 'ne'er'
empathy	identifying with a character in a literary work
end-stopped	line of poetry which ends with some form of punctuation, creating a pause
enjambement	run-on instead of **end-stopped** line of poetry, usually to reflect its meaning
epic	long narrative poem telling a tale of heroic achievements over a period of time, often related to national identity and with supernatural elements

epistrophe	a rhetorical figure by which the same phrase is repeated at the end of successive lines, e.g. 1.3.71–73
eponymous	(of a literary work) named after its main character, e.g. *Doctor Faustus*
fable	short fictitious tale conveying a moral, often involving animals or legendary figures
farce	improbable and absurd dramatic events to excite laughter
figurative	using imagery; non-literal use of language
foot/feet	division of syllables into a repeated metrical unit in a line of poetry
foreshadowing	arranging events and information so that later events are prepared for
form	the way a text is divided and organised, the shape of a text on the page
genre	type or form of writing with identifiable characteristics, e.g. tragedy
Gothic	originally medieval genre that contains violence, death, horror, the supernatural and the macabre
hamartia	from a Greek word meaning 'error' or 'flaw', this term is used to refer to the error of judgement or the moral flaw with which a tragic hero brings about his own tragedy
hubris	from a Greek word meaning 'insolence, arrogance', this term is used for the overweening self-confidence and ambition that leads to tragedy
iambic pentameter	verse with five **feet** of iambs, i.e. unstressed/stressed alternating syllables; tetrameter has four feet and hexameter has six (alexandrines)
imagery	descriptive language appealing to the senses; imagery may be sustained or recurring throughout texts, usually in the form of **simile** or **metaphor**
in medias res	beginning a text in the middle of an event or conversation, e.g. 4.2
intertextuality	relationship between one text and another
irony	language intended to mean the opposite of the words expressed; an amusing or cruel reversal of an outcome expected, intended or deserved; a situation in which one is mocked by fate or the facts
juxtaposition	placing side by side for (ironic) contrast of interpretation
legend	story about a historical figure which exaggerates his or her qualities or feats
lexis	term used in linguistics to designate the vocabulary of a

	language, or sometimes the vocabulary used in a particular text
lyrical	of writing, expressing strong feelings, usually love; suggestive of music
malapropism	misuse of word in mistake for one resembling it, e.g. 'gridirons' for 'guilders' (1.4.31–32)
metaphor	suppressed comparison implied not stated, e.g. 'this feeds my soul' (2.3.157)
metonymy	substituting an attribute for the thing itself, e.g. 'age' for the Old Man (5.1.75)
metre	regular series of stressed and unstressed syllables in a line of poetry
miracle plays	medieval dramatic representations of Biblical stories or legends of saints; performed in towns after which they were named, e.g. York, and performed principally on feast days
morality plays	late medieval dramatic works with didactic purpose and including personified vices and virtues as characters; best-known example is *Everyman*
muse	the Muses were nine Greek goddesses who were the daughters of Zeus and Mnemosyne ('memory'). Each presided over on activity or art. It was traditional for a poet to invoke the aid of a particular muse to help him with his work
myth	fiction involving supernatural beings which explains natural and social phenomena and embodies traditional and popular ideas
narrative	connected and usually chronological series of events to form a story
parody	imitation and exaggeration of style for purpose of humour and ridicule
pathos	evocation of pity for a character in a situation of suffering and helplessness
personification	human embodiment of an abstraction or object, using capital letter or she/he, e.g. 'Hell calls for right' (5.1.49)
plot	cause-and-effect sequence of events caused by characters' actions
plurality	possible multiple meanings of a text
poetic justice	appropriate and often ironic rewarding of virtue and punishment of evil
protagonist	the principal character
psychomachia	compound of two Greek words, this term refers to the conflict of virtue and vice in a battle for the soul
pun	use of word with double meaning for humorous or ironic effect, e.g. 'familiar' (1.4.26, 28)

register	form of speech shaped by social context, level of formality
Renaissance	originating in Italy, the revival of the arts and sciences under the influence of classical models in the fifteenth and sixteenth centuries in Western Europe
repartee	a ready and playful retort; witty banter
rhetoric	art of persuasion using emotive language and stylistic devices, e.g. triple structures, rhetorical questions
rhyme	repetition of final vowel in words at the end of lines of poetry
rhythm	pace and sound pattern of language, created by **metre**, vowel length, **syntax** and punctuation
risqué	audaciously bordering on the unseemly; bawdy
scansion	system of notation for marking stressed (á) and unstressed (ǎ) syllables in a line of metrical verse
semantic field	group of words with thematic relationship, e.g. 'falling to', 'glutted', 'surfeits'
Seven Cardinal Virtues	faith, hope, charity, justice, fortitude, prudence and temperance
Seven Deadly Sins	the medieval Catholic Church preached that these sins were mortal and led straight to Hell: pride, envy, gluttony, lechery, avarice, wrath, sloth
simile	comparison introduced by 'as' or 'like', e.g. 'draw up Faustus like a foggy mist' (5.2.83)
soliloquy	speech by character alone on stage which reveals his or her thoughts
style	selection and organisation of language elements, related to genre or individual user of language
symbol	object, person or event which represents something more than itself, e.g. communion wine
syntax	grammatical arrangement of words and word elements in sentence construction
theme	abstract idea or issue explored in a text
tone	emotional aspect of the voice of a text
tragedy	literary work of a serious nature traditionally concerning people in high positions, with a fatal conclusion for both the guilty and the innocent; characterised by waste, loss and a fall from power
tragic hero	a literary character who makes errors in judgement in his actions, that inevitably lead to his own downfall
unities	three principles of dramatic composition, deriving from Aristotle, whereby a play should consist of one related series of actions, occur within one day and happen in one place
wit	intelligent verbal humour

Selected literary criticism

We read of one Marlin, a Cambridge scholar, who was a poet, and a filthy playmaker…hearken, ye brain-sick and profane poets and players, that bewitch idle ears with foolish vanities, what fell upon this profane wretch…Mark this, ye players, that live by making fools laugh at sin and wickedness.   (Edmund Rudierde, 1614)

I cannot find, in Marlowe's play, any proofs of the atheism or impiety attributed to him, unless the belief in witchcraft and the Devil can be regarded as such; and at the time he wrote, not to have believed in both, would have been construed into the rankest atheism and irreligion.   (William Hazlitt, 1820)

No sooner does he attempt the comic vein than his whole style collapses into mere balderdash.   (H. N. Hudson, 1872)

[Marlowe is] the father and founder of English dramatic poetry. [Marlowe's characters are] day-dreams of their maker's deep desires; projected from the men around him; and rendered credible by sheer imaginative insight into the dark mysteries of nature.   (J. A. Symonds, 1884)

It is impossible to call Marlowe a great dramatist…Marlowe was one of the greatest poets in the world whose work was cast by accident and caprice into an imperfect mould of drama.   (George Saintsbury, 1887)

Marlowe, the moment the exhaustion of the imaginative fit deprives him of the power of raving, becomes childish in thought, vulgar and wooden in humour, and stupid in his attempts at invention…itching to frighten other people with the superstitious terrors and cruelties in which he does not himself believe.   (George Bernard Shaw, 1896)

This excellent Faustus is damned by accident or by predestination; he is browbeaten by the devil and forbidden to repent when he has really repented. The terror of the conclusion is thereby heightened; we see an essentially good man, because in a moment of infatuation he had signed away his soul, driven against his will to despair and damnation.   (George Santayana, 1910)

The verse accomplishments of *Tamburlaine* are notably two: Marlowe gets into blank verse the melody of Spenser, and he gets a new driving power by reinforcing the sentence period against the line period. The rapid long sentence, running line into line,…marks the certain escape of blank verse from the rhymed couplet, and from the elegiac or rather pastoral note of Surrey,…

In *Faustus* Marlowe went farther: he broke up the line, to a gain in intensity, in the last soliloquy; and he developed a new and important conversational tone in the dialogues of Faustus with the devil.   (T. S. Eliot, 1919)

The limitless desire, the unbridled passion for the infinite, a certain reckless, high confidence in the will and spirit of man are all there [in Faustus's mind]. This rare power of abstracting the nature of man, of revealing only the universal and the general, yet so revealing it that it comes home to the heart of every individual man, reaches its height at the end of the play… [*Doctor Faustus* is] perhaps the most notable Satanic play in literature.   (Una Ellis-Fermor, 1927)

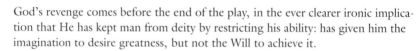

God's revenge comes before the end of the play, in the ever clearer ironic implication that He has kept man from deity by restricting his ability: has given him the imagination to desire greatness, but not the Will to achieve it.

(Nicholas Brooke, 1952)

Faustus moves repeatedly through a circular pattern, from thinking of the joys of heaven, through despairing of ever possessing them, to embracing magical dominion as a blasphemous substitute.

(C. L. Barber, 1964)

There is a case for seeing this devalued section of the play [the middle scenes] as an extraordinary phantasmagoria, grotesquely satirical, sometimes sinister, sometimes absurd, an illusionistic impression of twenty-four wasted years as bold in what it attempts theatrically as the scenes on the heath in *King Lear*.

(Malcolm Kelsall, 1981)

Doctor Faustus is neither a morality play nor an unambivalent celebration of radical humanism; it is a tragedy which dramatises a conflict between two irreconcilable systems of values, each of which, we may feel, has at least partial validity and a genuine claim to our allegiance. While Marlowe may have sympathised with Faustus's rejection of traditional authorities and the strict limits which they impose upon human aspirations, he was nonetheless aware that Promethean self-assertion could degenerate into debasing forms of self-aggrandisement.

(John S. Mebane, 1989)

The comic scenes form an integral part of the play because they question Faustus's actions. They may contain blasphemy, for instance when Wagner mocks the blessing, and yet they still manage to suggest orthodox responses to Faustus's contract with Lucifer.

(Roger Sales, 1991)

The play is about the struggle between the two sides of Doctor Faustus, the controlled intellectual side giving way in what may be seen as a mid-life crisis to the indulgent sensual. When the latter is in the ascendant, he betrays his ideals of pursuing knowledge. His manner is jocose and exuberant, his antics ludicrous or mad buffoonery, and he is driven by ambition. He pursues riches and pleasure, as if acting out day-dreams, but the demands he makes are seen by Mephistopheles as 'frivolous'; what he achieves is trivial. He over-reaches himself, his ambition for rich rewards and power driving him into wild, dangerous and ultimately tragic actions.

(Derek Russell Davis, 1997)

Today, significantly, *Faustus* on stage can be as powerfully moving for atheists and non-Christians as for orthodox Protestants or Catholics, since it does not depend on our attitudes to a creed.

(Park Honan, 2005)

Questions & Answers

LITERATURE

Essay questions, specimen plans and notes

Coursework titles

There are different styles of coursework titles depending on which board you are studying for. Your teacher will guide you to an appropriate format, but here are some suggestions for topics to explore.

1   Overreachers: Marlowe's *Doctor Faustus*, Shakespeare's *Macbeth*, Arthur Miller's *All My Sons*.

2   Magic and the supernatural: Marlowe's *Doctor Faustus*, Shakespeare's *The Tempest*, critical comment.

3   The battle for man's soul: Marlowe's *Doctor Faustus*, John Bunyan's *The Pilgrim's Progress*, *Everyman* (morality play).

4   The importance of the Chorus in Renaissance drama: Marlowe's *Doctor Faustus*, Shakespeare's *Henry V*, critical comment.

Exam essays

The suggested essay questions that follow can be used for planning practice and/or full essay writing, for classroom timed practice or for homework. They are based on the various styles of questions set by the different boards. It is important to check which Assessment Objectives you need to cover, as the boards have different requirements. You will find some essay titles with suggestions for ideas to include in a plan, and there are some with guidance from the board on how to approach the question. Sample student answers are provided for two of the questions.

Whole-text questions

AQA questions

Altogether, in Unit 3, AQA requires you to write two essays on three of the prescribed texts, all chosen for the theme 'Elements of the Gothic'. In Section A, you must answer a question on one text.

1   **What have you found striking about Marlowe's presentation of Mephistopheles and Hell in *Doctor Faustus*?**

Suggested content (from AQA Sample Assessment Materials)
Candidates might consider:
- how Marlowe constructs a sense of the character and appearance of Mephistopheles and of the nature of Hell

- the extent to which both might reflect period stereotypes of 'devils' or of Hell as a location
- Marlowe's purpose in adopting a 'traditional' moral/religious framework for the play
- other contextual and dramatic influences
- potential modern readings and significances

2   **Explore the dramatic use Marlowe makes of the occult and supernatural elements in *Doctor Faustus*.**
(Note: see sample essay 1 below for a response to this question.)

3   **Discuss the view that, in *Doctor Faustus*, Marlowe's main interest is not in morality but in the psychology of despair.**

Possible essay plan
- Explicit focus + warning to audience, implicit focus + way F creates for himself Hell on earth.
- (1.1.168) F thinks danger is of dying, no awareness of psychological danger. However, (2.1.1–9) before contract, trying to banish despair.
- (2.3) After contract needs 'sweet pleasure' to conquer deep despair – thinks too late to repent. Lucifer banishes despair until 4.1.128.
- Old Man, like Good Angel = voice of morality, but makes F despair. Paradox: 'Hell calls for right' – F is honourable, turning to God = breaking promise, so demoniality with H puts F beyond forgiveness, removes temptation.
- In final soliloquy F tries to repent but is prevented. Despair = longing for total annihilation of soul.
- Conclusion: Chorus, Old Man, Scholars + Good Angel emphasise morality, BUT power of poetry emphasises man who thinks he is beyond redemption. Marlowe explores various attempts to fend off despair + tortured efforts in final soliloquy to avoid eternal damnation.

4   **Discuss the view that, in *Doctor Faustus*, Marlowe manages to combine a sermon on the sin of pride with a celebration of aspiration.**
(Note: see sample essay 2 below for a response to this question.)

Comparative questions
In Unit 3 Section B, AQA offers you a choice of three questions. All questions will require you to compare elements of the Gothic across three texts that you have studied. In your responses to this paper you must write about at least one text written between 1300 and 1800.

1   **'Gothic texts show the supernatural intertwined with the ordinary.' Discuss this view in relation to the texts you have been studying.**

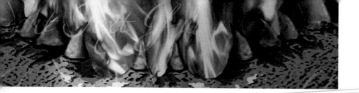

Suggested content (from AQA's Sample Assessment Materials)
Candidates might consider:

- what might be identified as 'supernatural' and 'ordinary' in their three chosen texts
- how such identification is open to interpretations via different cultural meanings of the key terms 'supernatural'/'Gothic'/'ordinary'
- what roles these elements play in the texts' structure
- what aspects of the texts' contextual backgrounds account for their presence
- how contemporary contexts impinge on the notion of the supernatural

2   **'Gothic literature is concerned with the breaking of normal moral and social codes.' Discuss.**

Suggested content (from AQA's Sample Assessment Materials)
Candidates might consider:

- the extent to which characters in their chosen texts illustrate actions that go against 'normal' behaviour or break boundaries set by God and/or man
- how notions of normality are cultural and so open to dispute
- the ways in which the plots enact a challenge to social convention
- the reader's response to these moral/social conflicts and possible other responses
- contextual influences, both of production and reception

3   **'If a text is to be labeled as Gothic, it must convey a sense of fear and terror.' Discuss this view in relation to the texts you have been studying.**

Suggested content (from AQA's Sample Assessment Materials)
From their three chosen texts, candidates might discuss and illustrate:

- fear/terror within the text itself and potential fear/terror for readers
- the near farcical extremes of fear/terror that Gothic sometimes has/is it frightening or is it funny?
- suspense + how it is created — and whether its impact has dimmed over time
- anticipation and chronology more generally
- delay/withholding of information: difference between reader knowledge and character knowledge
- the effect of narrative perspective and point of view
- dramatic/verbal/descriptive power
- the writer's sense of his/her audience: the possible interpretations of a contemporary readership.

4   **'The language of Gothic literature is usually inflated and melodramatic.' Discuss this generalisation in relation to the texts you have been studying.**

5   **'Gothic literature is characterised by sinister happenings and a sense of doom, sometimes supernatural, sometimes the product of wickedness.' Discuss.**

6   'One prominent feature of Gothic literature is terror, both psychological and physical.' Discuss this view in relation to the texts you have been studying.

WJEC questions: Shakespeare and Related Drama

Comparative questions: closed text (1 hour 15 minutes)

In Unit 4: WJEC offers you a choice of two questions on your 'core' Shakespeare text, *The Tempest*, which you have studied in detail, and *Doctor Faustus*, your 'partner' drama text, which you are required to study for wider reading.

1   **Examine the importance of magic in *The Tempest*.**
    Show how your appreciation and understanding of this aspect of *The Tempest* have been informed by your study of *Doctor Faustus* and critical readings of both plays.

Suggested content (from WJEC's Sample Assessment Materials)

Candidates may take a variety of approaches that could include the following:

- 'black' and 'white' elements of magic
- sources of magical power — Christian and pagan contexts
- creative and destructive uses
- magic as a structuring device for plot and characters
- how magical powers and events shape the course of the dramas
- moral issues surrounding supernatural powers
- the language and imagery of magic
- Renaissance notions of legitimate and forbidden knowledge
- magic within the context of a hierarchical society

2   **How does Shakespeare make dramatic use of the minor characters in *The Tempest*?**
    Show how your appreciation and understanding of the dramatic roles of three or four characters have been informed by your study of *Doctor Faustus* and critical readings of both plays.

Suggested content (from WJEC's Sample Assessment Materials)

Candidates may take a variety of approaches which could include the following material:

- discussion of the nature/dramatic qualities of minor characters
- consideration of theatrical traditions, e.g. types from morality plays
- use of minor characters in supporting development of main characters
- used to illustrate/reinforce themes
- devices for plot development/linking episodes and links with audience
- authors' comic and/or satirical purposes
- language and behaviour of minor characters reflecting plays' cultural contexts

3   **Explore the character of Prospero in *The Tempest*.**
    Show how your appreciation and understanding of the dramatic role of the central

protagonist has been informed by your study of *Doctor Faustus* and critical readings of both plays.

Possible essay plan

- Pursuit of unlimited knowledge leads both P and F into study of magic: P neglects responsibilities as Duke, F rejects conventional study.
- Neither can achieve much without spirits, however P thinks he has control over Ariel; F thinks he has control over M.
- M = servant to Lucifer but Ariel = bound to P by gratitude. A = airy spirit/malignant thing? — debate. M = fallen angel/ devil.
- P & F use magic to show off but P's magic is not demonic — its purpose is to care for Miranda (1.2.16). F actually invokes M and says he wants devils to obey him.
- Both proud of achievements, but P repents in time, drowns books, breaks staff. F despairs — gone too far to repent & only offers to burn books at end.
- F knows what his fate will be and when. P casts horoscopes & realises last chance. P under time pressure throughout play; F in final speech.
- Dramatic roles: P like a playwright, manipulating the other characters. F aspires to control but is manipulated by L & M.

4 **Examine the part played by comedy in *The Tempest*. Show how your appreciation and understanding of this aspect of *The Tempest* have been informed by your study of *Doctor Faustus* and critical readings of both plays.**

OCR questions: English Literature: Drama and Poetry pre-1800

Comparative questions: closed text (1 hour)

In your answer you must refer to one drama text and one poetry text from the list set and base your response on substantial discussion of both texts.

1 **By comparing one drama and one poetry text you have studied, discuss ways in which writers explore the dangers and delights of ambition.**

2 **By comparing one drama and one poetry text you have studied, discuss ways in which writers explore the idea of a personal hell.**

3 **By comparing one drama and one poetry text you have studied, discuss ways in which writers explore the concept of death.**

Possible essay plan

- F desires to defeat death — make men live eternally or raise dead to life. Rioters plan to defeat death because he kills so many, but neither act out of altruism.
- F is distracted by the potential of magic; rioters distracted by gold.
- F's first soliloquy establishes inevitability of death because man is sinful, so nothing to lose if you think Hell's a fable.
- P preaches repentance but does not think of it for self. Does not care about the soul

&, like F, seems to be gambling that Hell is a lie (like his sermons).

- P's story illustrates unpredictability of death (personified as adversary who betrays people), but predictable if you sin (Old Man predicts rioters' deaths).
- Rioters & F commit a mortal sin; gluttony (drunkenness) makes rioters hubristic & they seek Death. F is hubristic out of pride + gluttony for knowledge + power.
- Old Man in *DF* welcomes death because strong faith — believes flies to Heaven & 'celestial rest' + Old Man in *PT* wishes to die so bones at rest.
- F thinks 'Christ did call the thief upon the cross', so time to repent. Young man in *PT* intends 'nevere to repente'. In both fear of death comes with age.
- By F's final speech it is not death he fears but eternal damnation. P (like a boy — a gelding) = arrogant — talks of 'myn absolucion' — no fears for afterlife.

4   **By comparing one drama and one poetry text you have studied, discuss ways in which writers explore the theme of appearance and reality.**

5   **By comparing one drama and one poetry text you have studied, discuss ways in which sympathy is created for an unlikely protagonist.**

Sample essays

Sample essay 1

Explore the dramatic use Marlowe makes of the occult and supernatural elements in *Doctor Faustus*.

Records show that *Doctor Faustus* was an immediate success because of the dramatic nature of the supernatural elements, especially the devils. Audiences have always loved to be terrified, as long as they can enjoy the horrors from a safe distance. The terrifying apparition of Mephistopheles, whom Faustus judged 'too ugly to attend on me', as well as the 'terrible' aspect of Lucifer and Beelzebub who arrive just as Faustus begins to repent, would have evoked the delicious horror that persuaded audiences to put money in the hat in advance of their entrance.

Although the devils would all have looked grotesque, Baliol and Belcher would have made the audience laugh as they chased Robin around the stage and probably through the audience as well. Even the devil dressed as a woman that Mephistopheles gives Faustus for a wife could have been amusing after the initial shock. Marlowe pushes this delightful horror to its limit, however, by having Faustus actually conjuring Mephistopheles on stage. For an audience who believed in devils, this was a risky thing to do, and at some performances people were convinced that a real devil had appeared and, as one, the whole theatre emptied. Even if attempts to use supernatural elements dramatically did not chase the audience away, it would have made them look around fearfully.

The conjuring scene itself is grippingly dramatic. Performances would have been held in daylight, so Marlowe had to create a spooky atmosphere with Faustus's description of midnight, when 'the gloomy shadow of the earth…dims the welkin with her pitchy breath'. These words from the semantic field of darkness, together with the 'drizzling look' of Orion, would have created a tense, expectant atmosphere in the theatre. Then Faustus actually declares his intention to 'try if devils will obey thy hest' and proceeds to carry out the blasphemous ritual to force the spirits to rise. Faustus has to tell himself to 'fear not' and 'be resolute', clearly sending out messages of his own apprehension.

There follows a long incantation in Latin, a language that most of the audience would not understand, sprinkled with the names Beelzebub, Demogorgon, Jehovah and Gehenna, which they would recognise. To raise the tension even further, Faustus pauses in the middle of the speech, before asking '*Quid tu moraris?*' ('Why do you delay?') For those who did understand the Latin, it would have been even more frightening as he rejects the Holy Trinity and renounces his Christian baptism by misusing holy water and forswearing the vows made at his christening. The climax brings a horribly ugly apparition on stage, and the tension breaks as Faustus sends it away to return as a Franciscan friar, a joke that the Protestant audience would have appreciated.

Roman Catholics were the Queen's enemies, plotting to remove her from the throne and replace her with a Catholic monarch, and so they were popular targets for stage humour. Marlowe exploits this further in a scene at the Vatican where Faustus dons the traditional device of an invisibility cloak to play silly tricks on the Pope. However, even this farcical scene would have had its tensions, since, even though he is the head of a rival Church, the Pope is still a representative of Christ, and his humiliation would have created fear in the audience since he is so helpless and vulnerable to the forces of evil. The friars curse Faustus, but he is already going to Hell so they are powerless.

The scene ends in general mayhem as Faustus and Mephistopheles 'beat the friars, and fling fireworks among them'. The audience must have been relieved to see Robin and Rafe come on stage for a comic scene. They were not allowed to relax for long, however, as Robin imitates Faustus and pretends to read one of his spells. Although he remembers the words incorrectly, he conjures up an angry Mephistopheles who invokes Lucifer in an impressive speech. He reverses the iambic foot at the beginning of the first line to stress Lucifer's power — 'Monarch of hell'. Then he uses two heavy stresses at the beginning of the next line to emphasise how he makes 'Great potentates…kneel with awful fear', implying that, if powerful monarchs are filled with awe and fear by Lucifer, how much more terrified should mere servants be. Since most of the audience would be ordinary people like Robin and Rafe, the warning also applies to them.

Marlowe has made extensive dramatic use of the occult and supernatural elements in the play to create tension, raise laughs and arouse delightful horror, culminating in the devils who accompany Faustus to Hell at the end. No doubt there was an appropriately lurid representation of the mouth of Hell gaping to receive him in the inner stage. For a modern audience, however, it is neither the sets, nor the devils, nor the magic tricks that provide the dramatic tension. We are more likely to be transfixed by the psychological portrait of a man who believes in the occult and the supernatural, and who is finally reduced to begging that his soul 'be changed into little water drops', as he thinks he sees the angry face of God looking fiercely on him.

Sample essay 2

Discuss the view that, in *Doctor Faustus*, Marlowe manages to combine a sermon on the sin of pride with a celebration of aspiration.

From the very first speech of the play, the Chorus conveys a clear moral message that Faustus is punished for the deadly sin of pride. In the Prologue we are told that Faustus is 'swoll'n with cunning of a self-conceit'. He is still a young man, 'base of stock', like Everyman in the morality plays, and yet he has so excelled at university that he has been awarded a doctorate in divinity. He has 'glutted' himself on learning and now 'surfeits' upon 'cursed necromancy'. The vocabulary from the semantic field of over-eating links his desire for knowledge with base human appetites and links him with the deadly sin of gluttony. However, Faustus thinks he is going to try his brains to 'gain a deity'. The Prologue warns the audience that Faustus is too proud of his academic success, and, like Icarus who flew too close to the sun with his 'waxen wings', Faustus will be punished. We are even told that 'melting heavens conspired his overthrow', giving a clear indication that, although he has free will, God has fore-knowledge of what he will do and is preparing to punish him.

Throughout the play there are allusions to other legendary characters who desired more than they were permitted and were punished. Actaeon lusted after the goddess Diana and was turned into a stag; Semele desired to see her lover, Zeus, in his divine glory instead of disguised as a human, and she was struck by lightning. These references serve to remind us that Faustus is an overreacher, and the Epilogue confirms this strongly. We are commanded to 'Regard his hellish fall' and warned against 'such forward wits' who 'practise more than heavenly power permits'.

This sounds like a sermon on the sin of pride, warning us to be content with our allocated position in the Great Chain of Being, and the warning has been strongly reinforced by the sight of Faustus being taken to Hell by devils through a gaping mouth, which was one of the props used in morality plays. However, Marlowe has carefully made the ending ambiguous because the Chorus seems to be encouraging 'forward wits' like Faustus and Marlowe himself, to 'wonder at unlawful things', and the play has also strongly evoked a sense of wonder at the possibilities to which the human mind can aspire.

In Faustus's first soliloquy, Marlowe shows his hero being entranced by thoughts of what he will gain, leading up to power over absolutely everything. His list of five abstract nouns in 'a world of profit and delight,/ Of power, of honour, of omnipotence' ends triumphantly on a polysyllabic, Latinate word with a lingering feminine ending. This speech embodies the spirit of the Renaissance mind. It expresses the belief of occult philosophers that the possibilities open to the man who succeeds in the study of magic stretch 'as far as doth the mind of man'. Faustus lyrically declares that 'Necromantic books are heavenly', using religious lexis that suggests that he believes, like Paracelsus, that natural magic was the first stage of an aspiration to divine wisdom. He declares, 'A sound magician is a mighty god', and Marlowe has placed the evocative word 'god' in a prominent position at the end of a line and of a sentence.

Faustus, however, rejects God when he conjures the devil, Mephistopheles. When he realises his error and despairs, he is too proud to ask for God's mercy. He ignores messages sounding in his ears that say 'Abjure this magic, turn to God again!' and he declares 'To God? He loves thee not'. Throughout the play, he ignores all those who tell him that 'God's mercies are infinite', and he arrogantly decides for himself that 'Faustus' offence can ne'er be pardoned'. The play is like a sermon offering salvation through Christ to those who repent; the Old Man claims to see an angel hovering over Faustus offering to pour divine grace into his soul, but Faustus remains too proud to ask for it.

Although the play does act like a sermon on the sin of pride, the memorable speeches that we take away from the theatre are ones that celebrate the possibilities of the study of the occult arts. The most famous speech is the one in which Faustus marvels at the beauty of the succubus who appears as Helen of Troy, wondering 'Was this the face that launched a thousand ships/ And burnt the topless towers of Ilium?' However, even here, Marlowe is reminding the audience that seeking after this forbidden beauty will lead to the destruction of Faustus's aspirations, just as it led to the burning of Troy with its topless towers symbolising limitless ambition. Like Paris, Faustus desired Helen against all advice and wisdom; like Paris, he tried to take the forbidden, not only in the form of Helen but also in seeking divine knowledge.

Marlowe does manage to celebrate human aspiration and write lyrical poetry that speaks to the audience of the infinite possibilities open to us. The framework of a morality play gave him the freedom to explore unorthodox ideas and at the same time to appease the censor with warnings against the dangers. All the heresies are spoken by a devil or by a man whom we eventually see being carried off to Hell. However, although he gives Faustus memorable poetry in which to express his aspirations, there is little evidence that he actually achieves anything more than flying in a chariot drawn by dragons and an embrace with a spirit in the form of the most beautiful woman who ever lived. As a hero, Faustus is disappointing because he is so easily sidetracked from his ambitions into playing silly tricks.

Further study

History

Mebane, J. S. (1989) *Renaissance Magic and the Return of the Golden Age*, University of Nebraska Press

Tillyard, E. M. W. (1943) *The Elizabethan World Picture*, Peregrine Books

Biographies

Hoffman, C. (1956) *The Murder of the Man Who Was Shakespeare*, Julius Messner

Honan, P. (2005) *Christopher Marlowe: Poet and Spy*, OUP

Riggs, D. (2004) *The World of Christopher Marlowe*, Faber and Faber

Criticism

Cheney, P. (ed.) (2004) *The Cambridge Companion to Christopher Marlowe*, CUP

Davis, D. R. (1997) *Scenes of Madness: A Psychiatrist at the Theatre*, Routledge

Jump, J. (ed.) (1969) *Marlowe: Doctor Faustus*, Casebook series, Macmillan

Levin, H. (1961) *Christopher Marlowe: The Overreacher*, Faber

Sales, R. (1991) *English Dramatists: Christopher Marlowe*, Macmillan

Magazine articles

Austen, G. (September 2003) 'The strange ambiguity of Christopher Marlowe and *Dr Faustus*', *The English Review*

Cash, P. (February 1997) 'Living hell', *The English Review*

Ingles, H. (April 2006) 'Dr Faustus and the language of power', *The English Review*

Websites

Images

http://atheism.about.com/od/christianhistory/ig/Seven-Deadly-Sins-Punishments/Deadly-Sin-Pride-Punishment.htm

- The first in a series of seven medieval woodcuts depicting the punishments expected for the Seven Deadly Sins.

http://farm3.static.flickr.com/2088/2165878985_9cafeae597.jpg

- A picture of the Swan Theatre drawn by Johannes de Witt in 1596.

www.godecookery.com/macabre/macabre.htm

- Supernatural and fantastic imagery of the Middle Ages.

http://mimnir.org/kat/imgs/hellmouth.jpg

- A medieval picture of the mouth of Hell.

Sound

www.open2.net/drfaustus/index.html

- An extremely useful resource. A web link to an excellent audio-recording of the play, as well as interviews with some of the cast.

Useful resources

http://weblingua.hostinguk.com/invictaweb/canterburybuildings/index.htm

- The homepage of a website about Canterbury with links to maps, including one drawn in about 1580, photographs of carvings on buildings, including King's School, and photographs.

www.marlowe-society.org

- The website for the Marlowe Society.

www.luminarium.org/renlit/marlowe.htm

- General information about Marlowe and his work plus excellent links to other sites.

Films

1967: directed by Richard Burton and Nevill Coghill, starring Richard Burton and Andreas Teuber